The Hawaiians

The

Produced by Island Heritage Limited

Directed and photographed by Robert B. Goodman

Text by Gavan Daws and Ed Sheehan

Designed by Harry Williamson

Edited by Jonathan Rinehart

AN ISLAND HERITAGE LIMITED BOOK

Hawaiians

Produced and published
by Island Heritage Limited,
Norfolk Island, Australia,
with offices at 7 Ridge Street,
Sydney, New South Wales, Australia

This edition first published in Japan in June 1970
and distributed by John Weatherhill, Inc., with
editorial offices at 6-13 Roppongi 7-chome,
Minato-ku, Tokyo

Fourth printing November 1970

Distributed in the Hawaiian Islands
by W. W. Distributors Limited, 1132 Auahi Street,
Honolulu, Hawaii 96814

Distributed in the continental United States and Canada
by Walker and Company, 720 Fifth Avenue,
New York, N.Y. 10019

Library of Congress Catalog Card Number 77-118012

Engraving, printing, and binding by
Nissha Printing Co., Ltd., Kyoto

Set in 12 pt Monotype Bembo Series 270
by Dover's Pty Ltd, Sydney, Australia

To those who would be children of the land

Contents

I Origins

Living in limitless June, our senses make substitutes for the seasons. We know wonders of pasteled coral clusters, our world is necklaced with surf-strings. We move among soft, sudden rain caresses and our lives are stippled with ginger flower scents and briny surf tastes. Behind us ropy waterfalls cascade thousands of feet to overflow the deep, dark valley pools, to wander and feed the fertile earth and, shimmering over pebbled shallows, to make music on their fretted journey to the sea.

Living on isolated islands, we cherish our diversities. For we have come from many places and in many different ways to this enormous yet intimate chamber of summer.

It all begins with journeying. The visitor flies in search of the sun across the time zones, and his first discovery is that his biological clock has gone wrong. He leaves the jet feeling as if his soul is still strapped in the seat. He has lost his guide book and he cannot trust his senses. The welcoming smile seems real, but isn't the welcoming lei plastic? All the way in from the airport it is used car lots and pizza parlors, and he has seen those before. From the hotel he is likely to see another hotel. If he is luckier he manages a private panorama, but even this looks two-dimensional because he has seen it before as well – on picture postcards. The first night he drinks and dines by torchlight. But as the tradewinds shift, the torch blows kerosene smoke in his face, and the brown-skinned girl with a flower in her hair, serving him a Missionary's Downfall in the dusk with the light behind her, turns out to be a Southern Californian recently transplanted. He feels he has come a long way and arrived ... where?

He sleeps badly, dreams unsuitably of the mating of elephants and wakes to the pounding of a steam pile-driver outside his window: it is building still another hotel. On the beach he dozes again. The sand is warm, the waves make small comforting sounds. He wakes, and the sky is an improbable laundered blue above him. He lifts his head and catches sight of a profound green palm and in the distance a yearning amethyst mountain. He feels somehow different; he does not know why. He thinks, fearfully, that the sun must have poached his brain. Then he realizes that he has made a journey. He has arrived, his soul has caught up with him, and he is sure he will be happy every minute from now on for as long as he is an islander, even if it is only seventy-two hours.

Man, to be content, needs 160 square feet of sand (so the statisticians say, straight-faced). For instant paradise, add water. By such standards a man can be happy at Waikiki now, but only just. So well is Hawaii known among pilgrims to contentment that more than a million visitors come now each year, and the trend is steadily up. By 1985 there will be only fifty square feet of beach a man can call his own, and at that point presumably he will turn upon his basking neighbor and kick sand in his face. If the rate of increase is maintained till the year 2000 (say the statisticians, still straight-faced), the islands will have 2,150,000 visitors a day. How many of them will be able to dance on a grain of sand? It is a metaphysical question.

In the meantime, about 800,000 people actually *live* in the islands: Japanese, Chinese, Filipinos, Koreans, Puerto Ricans, Portuguese, every kind of European and American (Westerners usually go by a Hawaiian name – haole, meaning foreigner or stranger), and people of Polynesian ancestry. The first Hawaiians came a thousand years ago and more, by ocean-going canoe. Others have come since by China clipper and missionary bark and coolie transport, by cruise liner, freighter and troopship.

It was November of 1940 and we were 900 men on the way to work at Pearl Harbor.

It seemed the closer we came to the islands the cleaner and clearer the world became. A sunshower burst once, dropping pea-size pellets on water suddenly gone slack and smooth. And then a porpoise school appeared out of the ink, hundreds upon hundreds of bullet bodies with their bone-fixed smiles – hard, fast and sure, just under the surface, breaking the water and hanging in flying arcs for instants, backs glistening gunmetal. The men along the rail watched them in wonder, landbound men from Missouri, Ohio and Idaho. There were grunts of surprise and nervous laughs, as if men realized this was but a surface-flutter, bespeaking other and greater creatures unknown. And they fell into a curious quiet when the animals suddenly were gone.

The sea, the ship-world, returned to its silence under clouds and graying sky. We felt and heard only the shudder of great screws that churned beneath and aimed us at the horizon. A wind returned and the sea stirred into life in endless gentle chops of feathered waves. We were aware that birds had joined us, wheeling and dipping over the wake and someone said it was because we were nearing land, and we went to the rails again, smoking and looking in the direction where Hawaii would be in the morning.

Waking before dawn, I climbed as high on the ship as I could, wanting to be by myself. We moved around the purple swellings of Koko Head and Koko Crater, past the bowl of Diamond Head and along the brief ribbon of Waikiki. Inshore the indigo water swelled and turned into green over shallows. Long rollers built and tumbled into surf that raced toward the land. We could see a few buildings through trees along the shore, quiet and lifeless. The sun was behind the mountains and the sky a pale blue in dawning. The peaks of the Koolau range had a crisp, cool look, roughhewn and sharp in silhouette. I felt a pure peace was over the land. It slumbered sweetly, innocently, childlike. The streets on the hillsides, losing themselves in time against fluted valley walls, were still, and houses snuggled like toys against lush backdrops of growth.

The big ship eased into Honolulu harbor and bluntnosed tugs nudged us toward the pier. The buildings along the waterfront were quiet, as if the ship was not expected. Then husky brown men appeared and grinned up at us. They tugged at lines, making jokes we could not hear; only bursts of laughter lifted up to the men on deck. Over the wharf buildings I saw coconut palms for the first time. Their tufts moved gently in a light breeze, the thin fronds brushing each other affectionately. A black cannon sat on a triangle patch of grass, its muzzle pointed at a large dark stone building. The spire of Aloha Tower rose above us, a few pennants fluttered. And there was a perfume from the town – the morning smells of coffee, greenery and earth washed by night rain, mustiness of old wood from decrepit piers mixed with the aroma of blossoms not yet seen.

I thought, I am here, and it is what I wanted it to be.

You cannot help wondering, now that the voyagers are all here, where they thought they were going when they started out, and where they imagine they are now – whether some of them think they have come too far, or not far enough. A puzzlement, but one you are allowed, as long as you realize that it is only yours and not necessarily anyone else's.

The real Hawaiians, those with Polynesian blood, still do some of the things they used to do. They remain fond, for instance, of giving a child away and receiving another to bring up in return, without Oedipus or Electra but with love. Hanai is the word they use for them. "Kealoha is my brother's child," says the pleasant Hawaiian woman of the little girl she is raising as her daughter. "Of course my brother isn't really my brother as both he and I are hanai children of my father. I guess my father isn't really my father, is he? I know who my real mother is but I don't like her and I never see her. My hanai brother is half-Hawaiian and I am pure Hawaiian. We aren't really any blood relation I guess, but I always think of him as my brother and I always think of my father as my father. I think maybe Papa is my grandfather's brother; I am not sure as we never asked such things. So I don't know what relationship Kealoha really is though I call her my child." All this with no sense of strain on her part. Your puzzlement is not hers.

An elderly couple, tourists, nice people with bright shirts and clear eyes, tell you on a street in Waikiki that they are in from Fresno, raisin capital of the world, and that the Japanese have taken over the islands. They have just come from visiting a friend, a Californian who has lived in Hawaii for several years. He greeted them at the door barefoot, they said, and invited them to take off their shoes and make themselves at home. Certainly their puzzlement is not yours.

Japanese, native Hawaiians, and all the others here, including transplanted Californians – it cannot be that all their brains are addled. And yet perhaps the mild and magnificent sun has managed to take the edge off the collective asperity of mankind in the islands. Certainly the people of Hawaii get on extraordinarily well with each other, as things go in an imperfect world. These days, one in every three marriages crosses some racial or national line. The result is a population more and more mixed with each generation. "Cosmopolitan" is the local word, and it stands for a glorious puzzlement of a people. How can someone with three racial strains and a dozen national origins in his background explain himself to the census-taker? He is a Hawaiian, he says, as others are Californians or Texans or Iowans. But somehow not quite, or not yet, and he knows it. Just the same, he is an American, and he will insist on it. And he will be right, by birthright. Hawaii has been American soil since 1898, and a state of the union since 1959.

E pluribus unum, it says on the back of the coins. A capacious and generous definition. It allows – you will see – all sorts of Hawaiians to live under the American flag, and to be themselves. You will find them now in all shapes and sizes and colors. You will come upon them at meetings of the Elks or the ADA, shopping in the air-conditioned caverns of Sears and J. C. Penney's, dozing in front of television sets or watching beach birds in their bikinis, marching in the National Guard or with heads dipped over a Dow Jones ticker. You will also find them narrow-eyed and playing fan-tan in alleys, tying small knives to the legs of roosters, counting by abacus, eating raw fish, sitting crosslegged in teahouses, worshipping before Buddha.

Preceding page: Barquentine California,
with tourists, evening off Waikiki, Oahu.

Below left to right: Construction worker
building hotel; television cameraman covering
Hawaiian Open; steelmaker re-melting scrap metal;
countergirl at Honolulu supermarket.

Below left to right: Returning soldier
and wife, Honolulu; local fisherman,
Kailua, Kona; bather, Waikiki.
Far right: Tourists, Kalakaua Avenue, Waikiki, Oahu.

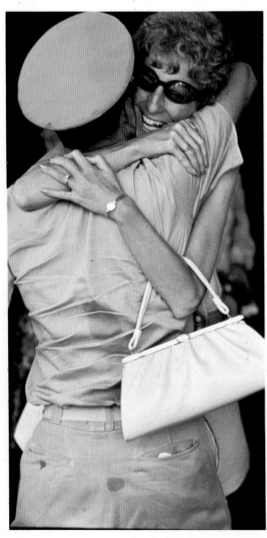

Like all who came before, we brought our big and little dreams, our prejudices, suspicions and hungers. We carried our talismans and trinkets – goodluck pieces, rosaries, Stars of David, Bibles and wallet snapshots. Some guarded their toolboxes as if they were precious portable altars.

There were those of us who loved it here from the first and have stayed. But out of the original 900 men on that ship, I'd guess that all but fifty have left in one way or another. Some were rock-hard tenement boys and rednecks who called the Hawaiians niggers. They saw and felt little outside the nightly crap games and the payday visits to the River Street whores. They saved for the stake and when they made it, they left.

We had all crawled through the depression of the 1930s. In many, it had left a harshness and sourness. This was truer of the older men, for their time was running out. Coming to Pearl and Hawaii meant little really, other than work and good pay after long and hungry years. The older men were first-class journeymen, rough and gruff, with a workman's suspicion of things that came too easily. Eternal summer for them was wrong somehow, too easy. They were aliens and always would be to island ways. They had no understanding of slant-eyed and brown local men – men who ate damp rice balls for lunch, spoke a pidgin English and fished for crabs from the docks.

For those whose minds run that way, the outlandish still abounds. But somehow things refuse to stay merely picturesque. A fisherman stands motionless on a reef, the throw net on his shoulder a nylon copy of the sennit snare woven by the ancient Hawaiians. Still as a sculpture, he waits for the water whorls to show him the moi and the akule. The scene composes itself beautifully. Then, behind him, a noisy motorboat tows a water skier across the line of vision, and all is lost.

The sensible man learns to cope with this, and becomes instead a connoisseur of reversed expectations. The Oriental on the sidewalk, classically inconspicuous, goes into a blocky building across from Iolani Palace, enters a phonebooth-sized closet, and emerges robed as a justice of the State Supreme Court. The householder who flies a gaily colored paper carp on Japanese Boys' Day is not, it turns out, Japanese. The Republicans at a party singing dirgelike choruses of "Danny Boy" for their defeated Irish gubernatorial candidate ("but come ye baaack") *are*, it turns out, Japanese.

The present pushes the past out of sight, and the past pushes back, everyday, everywhere. On a cliff trail a donkey edges along under the weight of wet bags of poi from taro patches in a quiet green valley; the paste will be packaged in plastic and sold in supermarkets. Just feet from a six-lane freeway a Japanese temple is being built, a replica of the famous original, exact down to one-sixty-fourth of an inch. A block from a new bank, noodles are made as they were in old Canton. The Chinese have taken over New Year. They have their lunar celebrations in Chinatown, with paper lions; but on everybody else's New Year's Eve as well, fireworks go off, millions of them; Honolulu sounds as if it is under siege. And not long ago, as the high point of the New Year, the Waikiki Junior Chamber of Commerce, which has a good many Japanese members, staged a simulated atom bomb explosion, complete with fireball and mushroom cloud. May we all live a thousand years.

It has all happened fast, almost too fast to comprehend. There used to be a tortoise living on the Kona Coast of the Big Island, Hawaii itself. Everybody knew him. He was supposed to have come ashore with the discoverer of the islands, Captain James Cook, who first landed in 1778. Between his slow tortoise's middle age and his slower old age, Hawaii ceased to be a primitive kingdom and became a constitutional monarchy; Hawaiians became Christians, or near enough; and Honolulu grew into one of the great ports of the Pacific. Before the tortoise died, in the 1860s, the first Oriental immigrants arrived to work on the sugar plantations that made Hawaii rich. And before the Japanese dwarfed and pruned their first bonsai tree to proper elegance, the Hawaiian kingdom fell to some quiet Anglo-Saxon revolutionaries, and the islands became American soil. In the 1920s the United States forbade the entry of any more Orientals, and about ten years after that again, an Oriental couple from Honolulu went for a visit to the Far East. The wife was pregnant, and she had her child, a son, away from home. Back at Honolulu, she was stopped by officials. They thought she was trying to smuggle a small illegal migrant ashore. "They put me in a cage," she says. "A cage! That's what is was – a wire cage – like an animal!" She tells the story in the penthouse suite of a twenty-story hotel her husband owns in Waikiki. Her son is in the state legislature. *E pluribus unum*.

We were quartered first in old houses that were dormitories before they built the new Kamehameha Schools up on the hill. The two-story rooming houses surrounded a base-ball field and the Bishop Museum buildings stood on the mountain end. On the first day, waiting for assignment to a room, I wandered over to the steps of the museum where there was an old Hawaiian standing with a young haole man. They wanted to know where we men had come from and what we were going to do. I told them we came from different states to work at Pearl Harbor. I asked them about the building and they told me it was the museum of Hawaii and the Pacific and I looked in the dark inside and it seemed like museums everywhere. There was a big map of the islands on the wall and they pointed out where we were, in Honolulu, on Oahu. I noticed first the soft touch the old man gave each vowel separately. "O-ah-hoo," he said and it sounded quite pleasant. I asked him to speak some Hawaiian for me and he smiled and said, "Aloha nui kakou," which means, "A big welcome to all of us."

The young haole smiled. He was a teacher at the school, he said, and was interested in all things Hawaiian. I asked if he could speak Hawaiian too. He rattled off, "Ua mau ke ea o ka aina i ka pono – The life of the land is perpetu-ated in righteousness," the motto of the Territory, words said by a king once in a speech. He showed me the inscription on a coat of arms and I copied it down, thinking to learn it – and more about this place and these people.

I smile now, remembering: on that first day I was writing a Hawaiian phrase.

The voice of the land had drawn and touched me, borne on sun-drunk trees, flower aromas, ease and warmth of people, clarities of mountain and sea. It was all so different from the Boston I left; yet I felt happy, safe, and quite at home. I was twenty-one and could not have known I would spend the rest of my life in the islands. I could not vision growing to know and love Hawaii even more as months moved into years. I was unaware that my curiosity would creep into eagerness for wandering, exploring and learning.

Left: Sunrise, approaching Laau Point,
south coast of Molokai.

Below: Morning, north coast of Molokai,
near Kalaupapa.

Below: Late afternoon clouds, north coast,
Island of Hawaii.

Right: Late afternoon rain shower,
Alenuihaha Channel, east of Kahoolawe.

Left: Sooty terns, late afternoon, Midway Island.
Above: Fairy terns, early morning, Midway Island.

That day, in the gloom of the museum entrance, I could not know that I would become, irrevocably and in my own way, a Hawaiian.

E pluribus unum. There is a secure place now for almost everyone in the islands. Except, a little sadly, for those who were here first. The ladies of the Kaahumanu Society, picking their way past the tour buses in front of Iolani Palace, are aged, brown, and wrinkled. They are dressed in black holokus, long-sleeved dresses that fall from throat to ankle. Around their necks are leis of orange feathers, and atop their heads are small-crowned, broad-brimmed black hats. Expressionless, they gather on a patch of lawn near the bandstand built by the last of their kings and bearing the emblems of his reign on its eaves. They are here for some reason of their own: the commemoration of a death, or the anniversary of another day when a piece of their Hawaii fell into foreign hands. They form scraggled ranks and sing in creaking contralto, aiming their voices at the columns of the palace, where three-quarters of a century ago the revolutionaries imprisoned their queen, and she sat at her window writing songs. The chorus is in Hawaiian, and the onlookers have no idea what it is. But people pause to look and listen, and they cannot help falling silent. For there is something terribly strong about this curious platoon of ancients. Singly, they are little old ladies in black. Together they command and dominate, these sacristans of the past. Once, after all, the whole ocean world was theirs.

While learned Europeans of the Middle Ages were still clinging, unweaned of fear, to the ancient comfort of continental coastlines, blocking off the borders of their fantastic faintheart maps with the dragons of the mind, the uninstructed islanders were out on the open sea in their double canoes, finding and settling, one after another, the scattered archipelagoes and atolls that made up the world of the Polynesians.

Even so, the islanders, the ancestral Hawaiians, were not the earliest visitors. The islands, less than 6,500 square miles of land in 70 million square miles of water, have been in existence long enough to be found over and over again, by design and by chance.

The golden plover, the kolea bird, has a calculated interest in Hawaii. Migrating flocks come down each year out of Alaska and Siberia. Each bird flies the 3,000 miles to his own particular sunny acre. He walks about with a calm proprietary air, until it is time to go north again in the Arctic spring for nesting. The kolea knows what he is doing, but other birds are less sure of themselves. Some who do not belong in the islands at all appear every so often. Godwit, gadwall duck, glaucous gull, baldpate, red-breasted merganser, bufflehead: even their names sound like mistakes.

Tagalog, Takahashi, Cho-sen and Chinaman's Hat; Tantalus, Texeira and Kapiolani, kaukau and Kalanianaole. That first year was a kaleidoscope of places and names, of scents, tastes and sounds that sang – a year dearer to me than any other because it was in freedom and youth.

I was thin and life-hungry, wandering Honolulu like a lost crane, gulping experience, swallowing beauty. Each day was two – the one on swingshift in the drydock at Pearl, molten-metal-rain, welder's arcs, bruises, grime, the Greek's soggy sandwiches – and the other fashioned of soft hours of sun and near-empty beaches.

Most of us younger fellows soon moved to Waikiki, for the same reasons young people do today. We rented rooms or little frame cottages in narrow lanes where great hotels now stand. The evenings were tender and dark then, with silences broken by ukuleles and girls' laughter, and street-lights filtering lace-shadows on near-empty sidewalks. Panax hedges were friendly fences of greenery between lanais. Sleep came sweetly and in the morning there was always the call of the flower-lady.

"FLAAAAAHR!"

It rang on silent air, an incongruously lonesome cry from one selling sprays of loveliness carried in wet cones of news-paper in a big basket atop her head. The flower-lady was a tiny old Japanese woman, wrinkled brown in faded cotton, with leather feet in sandals and she sold her brilliant bundles for a quarter. When you opened the door she smiled and bowed, the heart of dignity, ageless peasant grace.

And I remember an island girl who had a marvelous, exciting, limb-stretching shudder when she awoke. She was a delicacy in bronze, sleepy-eyed, silent and sex-sullen until her little smile came. Wonderfully, muskily woman-smelling from love, she would get a jar or milk bottle for the flowers and place them near us and we would lie there, not talking, as the flower lady paddled down the street.

"FLAAAAAHR!"

Hawaii offered world enough for life, and time for growth. It was a small world of its own, 2,000 miles or more from the nearest land masses in the north, farther again from the southern continents. Within the islands, there were other islands: of stillness on the highest mountaintops, of withdrawn peace in caves and gorges. And the most private of all, the kipukas, tiny beds of growth left isolated by lava flows and untouched, where life could go its intimate, experienced way, while on the raw rock alongside, the affair might start all over again – beginning and ending, this time, just a shade differently.

Evolution's castaways here were a strange group, with some notable absentees. Hawaii has no native land reptiles or amphibians, few freshwater fishes, only two kinds of native mammals (a bat and a monk seal), and only a third of the world's orders of insects.

Some of the early arrivals took the broad view of their situation. They found not much competition, and were able to expand their living range all over the islands. The Hawaiian tree snails went the other way, and chose exclusiveness. They live only on Oahu, Maui, Molokai and Lanai. There are hundreds of species, each with its own identifying whorled shell. Some inhabit only one valley or mountain ridge; some attach themselves to trees of a single species, and only to certain trees within the species and no others. That is one way of doing things, and the tree snail does not see much of the world.

New species of all kinds have proliferated amazingly. "I would give," said Charles Darwin, an interested observer, "£50 to any man who would collect for me at the Sandwich Islands." The money would have been well spent. It was birds from another set of islands, the finches of the Galapagos, which changed Darwin's notion of the world, and humanity's idea of itself. Remarkable; but the Hawaiian honeycreepers out-finched the finches before Darwin was ever heard of. They came, evidently, from North America. In the islands they found so many different sorts of places to

Right: Hawaiian tree fern, Tantalus, Oahu.
Far right: Silversword, Haleakala Crater, Maui.

Coconut and Loulu palms, sunset,
Kona Coast, Island of Hawaii.

live and adapted to them in so many ways – this bill-shape probing ever more surely into that food-source or mating ever more elegantly with that flower-form – that their common origin was all but obscured.

The native terrestrial biota of the Hawaiian chain – all the life of the land – numbers between 10,000 and 15,000 species, descended from perhaps a thousand original species. This means – in one of those calculations which outrun human scale and disappear down a corridor of zeros – that the original species established themselves perhaps at the rate of one every 20,000 years. For land mollusks, the rate is one establishment every 200,000 years; for land birds, with seventy native species all evidently descended from fifteen sorts of ancestors, it is once every 300,000 years.

You can still see the accidental landfalls being made. A solitary coconut, thousands of years late, bobs up from Tahiti or the Marquesas. A redwood log, barnacle-encrusted, drifts in from the American coast. Glass floats, beautiful things lost off Japanese fishing boats in the western Pacific, turn up tinkling in rock pools.

Eventually man had to take his chances on the broad Pacific. The Polynesians were the first to risk it, and what they managed is still hard to credit. Without maps or navigating instruments, they sailed and settled an enormous stretch of the loneliest waters in the world, the triangle of Polynesia, the place of many islands, reaching in the west to New Zealand, in the east to Tahiti, the Marquesas Islands, and Easter Island, in the north to Hawaii. White men have always been inclined to think of this accomplishment as somehow unreasonable. They do not like to think that savages could have done such things in the ordinary way. So the Polynesian has been made out to be either a superman, gifted with cosmic insight about islands, or a fool saved from wild incompetence on the ocean by lucky landfalls century after century.

After much passionate scholarly argument, it has become possible to say some commonsense things about the Polynesian and his migration to Hawaii. The general culture evidently has its origins in the western rather than the eastern Pacific; the major connections are with Asia rather than the Americas. The Hawaiian Islands were settled first from the Marquesas, a little less than 2,000 miles to the southeast, probably in the eighth century AD, perhaps somewhat earlier. A second wave of migrants, this time from Tahiti and the Society Islands, 2,200 miles to the south, came north between the twelfth and fourteenth centuries. Perhaps they made voyages back and forth between archipelagoes. Certainly they established the culture that the first white explorers found.

The valley was blustery with rain and wind, when I drove up to see the old woman, Kawena Pukui. There was a pout on the hills and clouds moved along the valley walls, low and heavy with wet. Yesterday, there had been lovely rainbows. Her house is at the end of the road, tucked under the cliffs and at the edge of a sharp slope to the valley floor.

Kawena has the loveliness of an old woman of sweetness and grace. Her hair is white, and face a light brown and wrinkled, a fine face with part-haole features, eyes alive and quick to smile with a small mouth. She was dressed in a loose house gown and it is apparent that she was once buxom and full in Hawaiian style.

Her father was Harry Wiggin, a seaman from Salem,

Massachusetts, but at birth her grandmother said to him: "Harry, this child is for me." Her father made no objection, knowing the Hawaiian style of hanai – the giving of children. So she was raised, knowing all the Hawaiian ways. Her father spoke Hawaiian fluently, but would speak only in English when addressing his daughter. She says he told a lot of stories but they were "New England stories." All the other stories she learned were from old Hawaiians.

She greeted me and we looked over the great floor of Manoa with its rooftops dull-glistening in the rain below. She said that she loved to look over the valley. It was never the same, always changing. And she pointed to places I had not noticed before.

"Ke awa Kii elei," she said. "The gulch of Kii. Named for a man who told lies about the Rainbow Maiden and was turned into a hill. These are kuahine, sister rains, we are having now. I sit here and enjoy watching them sweep over the land. And the rainbows yesterday moved so beautifully, starting low, then rising higher . . .

"Down there, the hill in the center, is called ka pali luahine, the old lady's hill. The legend is that the old lady came from far away, and lived here for a long time . . .

"Down this whole valley once there was an invisible line. The alii, the chiefs, lived on one side and the commoners on the other. Queen Kaahumanu died in this valley. Once there was a cistern down there, her own, the royal water bowl, huelani. That is the name of this street and I like it . . ."

The Polynesians were neither supermen nor fools, but they were fine seamen, as fine as any in the world, then or now. They had a serviceable canoe, double-hulled, high-prowed, big and sturdy enough to carry scores of people and tons of supplies. They had learned how to navigate by taking bearings on the rising and setting stars. They could estimate latitude by observing the zenith point of known stars. They could not estimate longitude with any accuracy, but they had the wit to sail to windward until they were in the latitude they wanted, and then come down the wind. Their first discovery of a group of islands would always be a matter of luck – what discovery is not? – but though one island might be just a dot in the ocean, the Hawaiian chain, hundreds of miles long, with cloud-capped mountains thousands of feet high, would offer reasonable odds on being found, over a period of time.

This is the white man's reconstruction of things. He manipulates the findings of linguists, folklorists, ethnobotanists, archeologists, anthropologists, and makes his string figures of theory.

The Hawaiian, for his part, says less. The elaborate legends which served the Polynesians for history in the old days are silent on the first migrations of the Marquesans. There are no canoe voyages from Tahiti to Hawaii and back any more, and there have not been for centuries; the navigating chiefs ceased to sail long before the first Western ships entered the Pacific. So it is mute evidence that speaks loudest. A fish hook unearthed in a cave on a Marquesan beach looks much like one picked from the ashes of a cooking fire that burned 1,000 years ago on the south point of Hawaii. And just south of Maui, you can sight out to sea along a channel that divides the small islands of Lanai and Kahoolawe. This stretch of water is called Kealaikahiki, the road to Tahiti. The strings of the puzzle are not yet worked into place. They stretch across 2,000 miles of open ocean still.

Left: Hawaiian god figure, Honaunau, Island of Hawaii.
Right: Moon over Mokulua Island, Lanikai, Oahu.

II Seasons

It is conceivable, in the vast scheme of things, that the islands might vanish tomorrow. There have been signs.

On Hawaii, the Big Island, in the spring of 1868, the great volcanoes of Mauna Loa and Kilauea erupted together. The whole island went into seismic spasm. Earthquake shocks coursed through the ground like rolling cannonballs for weeks on end. Along the coastal cliffs, millions of tons of rock broke loose and slid into the ocean. The sea rose and fell; waves fifty and sixty feet high crashed down on the beaches, carrying away entire villages. Men standing on dry land got seasick. In some places the ground shifted twelve feet along a fault line; brick houses collapsed in shambles, straw huts were shredded. Onto one valley a whole hillside of volcanic ash descended; rainsoaked, it came loose and slid down to bury a village and all its livestock.

The epicenter of the earthquake swarm was somewhere in the Ka'u district of southern Hawaii. A hundred miles away at the other end of the island, in Kohala, a seventy-five horsepower steam engine going full bore was stopped dead. In Honolulu, two hundred miles away on Oahu, pendulum clocks stopped ticking. The world has not seen many earthquakes more severe than that one. The seismic energy it released took something like 375,000 square miles of ocean to exhaust itself.

Will it happen again? Those who should know say yes, almost certainly, just as San Francisco will someday have another earthquake. Soon? The experts think there is a ninety percent probability of another major quake on Hawaii before the end of this century. Mauna Loa and Kilauea owe the world a warning, and they mutter incessantly. But no one knows what they are saying. They may be prophesying doom, they may be chanting the birth of new lands.

"Let more land grow from Hawaiki
From Hawaiki the birthplace of lands.
The quickened spirit of the dawn rides
Upon the flying scud beyond restraining bounds.
Bear thou on! Whence beats the drum?
It beats beyond in the western sea
Where the sea boils . . ."

Kawena Pukui comes from Ka'u, the southernmost point of Hawaii, where the land swells up from the sea like a mother's breast. That is what the people named Kawena's district, Ka'u, "the breast that nursed them."

I have often gone back to South Point, for this is where Hawaii ends – and is still being born. Below the flank of Mauna Loa, in the Ka'u and Puna areas, much of the land is a sere, vast lava desert and the loneliness is superb. The cindered tongue-tip of Ka Lae points toward Hawaiki, the legendary motherland, 2,000 miles distant over a forbidding, spray-whipped ocean. Here bassoon gales moan into sea caves through kiawe and coconut trunks and die whining in ragged gulches. Sea birds screech in impotent protest. Dry dead limbs crackle and drop to finality on the ash earth. Deep under the plateau, trickles of water struggle seaward, leach up through the porosity and give life to the kipukas, the thirsting oases of kiawe, coco palms and scrub brush in tiny islets. Even the holy temples and house platforms of the ancients are buried deep and not remembered, and the walking creatures – snaking mongoose, iron-muscled goat, half-mad stray cat and rib-skinned dog – are on constant prowl for a seeping of brackish water, a leaf, a food scrap.

One can travel to softer shores, and close by, to jade

pastures and velveted valleys through tree corridors that shut out the sun, to mountainsides long untouched by the volcano, to huge forestings of ironwood, pine, koa, and monkey pod that drip in cool rains. But at land's end on Hawaii, it is still the source, a genesis in rawness.

Beginnings and endings, endings and beginnings – on the brink of the fire pit the two become one. Quiescent, Mauna Loa lies cold and bare, a black breast nippled with snow. Kilauea, an immense, ash-rimmed, Cyclopean earth-eye, stares at the sun. Then, deep in the crater, the fontanel swells and heaves. The earth shudders and pants and roars. The breath of creation turns sulphurous, killing. Magma boils and blossoms, fire fountains play above the cinder cones. Rivers of molten stone breach the mountain flanks and course blood-red down the valleys, spreading deltas of disaster across the lowlands.

Sometimes the lava reaches the sea, and there, from a marriage veiled by clouds of steam, new land is born. In time, beaches of black sand come into being, unnaturally beautiful. Nothing much will grow on those dark dunes, and along the way good land has been burned into scar tissue and beautiful forests have been tumbled and consumed like sputtering matchsticks. But the volcano's touch can be perversely delicate. A tiny fern will leave in the lava a death-cast of itself, perfect down to the last filigreed vein and spore. Elsewhere the flow kills and embalms living trees in an instant and shrouds them in hardening rock – mad sculpture in a giant's graveyard.

Mauna Loa and Kilauea are prodigal. In less than a century they have erupted nearly a hundred times.

Once, Mauna Loa was active for almost a year at a stretch, and during the past hundred years it has released more than 3.5 billion cubic yards of lava. There are other volcanic mountains, big ones, close by – Hualalai, Kohala, and the highest of all, Mauna Kea. These are dormant now, or at least quiescent. And on the other major islands of the chain, strung out west-northwest across the Tropic of Cancer, only one volcano, Haleakala on Maui, closest to Hawaii, has erupted in historic time, and that was perhaps two centuries ago.

Every eminence in the archipelago is volcanic: the West Maui mountains, Haleakala's attendants; the Koolaus and the Waianaes on Oahu, and Koko Head and Punchbowl, and Diamond Head itself, the great profile; and Waialeale on Kauai, with its rainforest slopes and swamp-filled crater, the wettest spot on earth. Indeed, every piece of land along the oceanic Hawaiian Ridge, from the summit of Mauna Kea, 13,796 feet high, to the merest knuckle tip of rock, almost 2,000 miles and hundreds of reefs, shoals, and atolls away to the northwest, has a common origin in a fracture in the earth's crust, out of which, for more than 25 million years, volcanic magma has been oozing.

The fracture opened earliest in the northwest, near Kure and Midway. The first high islands appeared there. They and all the others that followed were formed by endless submarine eruptions, laying down shield after shield of new rock in water more than 15,000 feet deep, until at last they thrust themselves into the air. About 10 million years ago, volcanoes became active at the southeastern end of the fracture, bringing into existence the major islands of Niihau, Kauai, Oahu, Maui, Molokai, Lanai, Kahoolawe, and

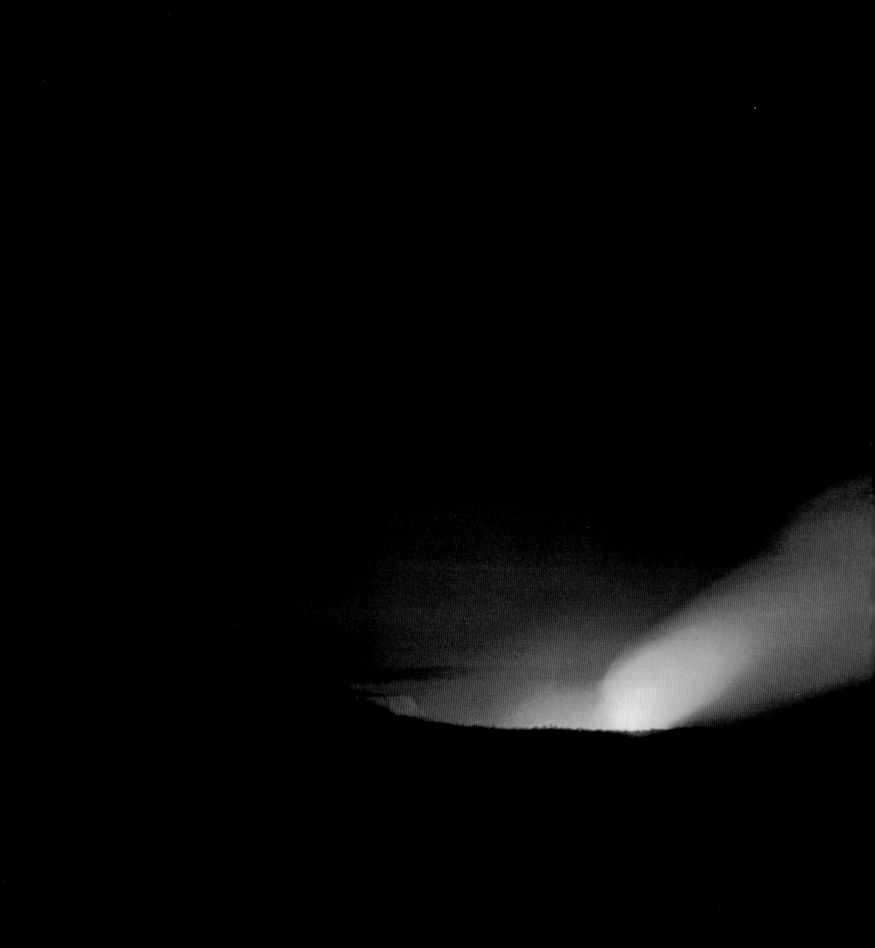

Kilauea eruption, Halemaumau Crater, Island of Hawaii.

Left: Kilauea Iki eruption near the vent,
Island of Hawaii.
Right: Kilauea Iki fountaining at dawn.

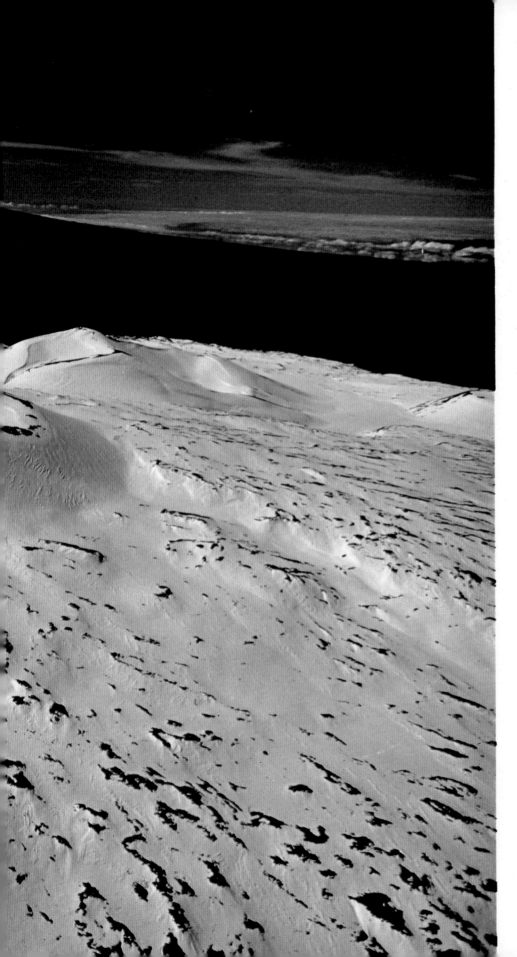

Mauna Kea summit, Mauna Loa behind,
Island of Hawaii.

– last of all – Hawaii. By then the calderas on Kure and Midway had capped themselves, and the ancient islands, weathered and eroded, sank slowly back into the sea under their own weight. Perhaps Midway was once as imposing as Mauna Loa and Mauna Kea, which are now more than 31,000 feet from ocean floor to summit, without much question the biggest mountains in the world. But today Midway's extinguished volcanic peak, coral-neckleted, then coral-crowned, and finally drowned again in salt water, is several hundred feet below the surface of the sea.

We came to Nihoa, some 250 miles northwest of Honolulu, on a large power cruiser, with every convenience. But stepping on the island, one steps back beyond time. You tramp dry grass and powder earth, peering into shallow cliff caves and over the stone platforms of houses long ago borne away on the winds. On Nihoa a drop of water is precious.

All that is left of the island is a peak shaped like a half saddle, sere and brown, a ragged speck of stone tortured by sun and sea. Cliffs rise 900 feet from the northern ocean. The southern side slopes about a half mile to rocky ledges.

The birds and the sea play a curious concerto. Except for them, it is quite still.

The birds are everywhere, tens of thousands of them, circling the sky, plummeting into black-blue water to feed, out to sea and back again. They flutter to scrub-covered stones to fill the squawking mouths of their young. Underfoot everywhere are the nesting terns, the frigates, bos'ns and boobies. Eggs crack open in the sun and the scrawny embryos peck, struggle and tremble into life. The fuzzy young are but heads and mouths, beaks open, quivering, screaming for food.

When Nihoa was first seen by Europeans in 1789 it was uninhabited by man. Nothing has changed since. It is a land chip of utter isolation. Two valley cliffs hold stands of loulu palm, found only on Nihoa. Birds exist here that live only at this world's end, and the opihi, delicious limpets much prized, grow to the size of small saucers.

Yet man once lived here too. There are worshipping maraes almost exactly like those of Tahiti and the Marquesas, and we picked a piece of charcoal from deep in a sheltered firepit of white ashes. Later it was carbon-dated. The man on Nihoa cooked his fish around 890 AD–at the time the Byzantine Empire was flowering. Perhaps the ancients came here to die. The sun sets in the west, and Nihoa is a sunset place.

No man saw Nihoa grow old, or Midway rise and fall. And no man has yet seen with his own eyes the newest seamounts of all, taking shape underwater south and east of Oahu and Hawaii. They may never reach the surface. Mauna Loa and Kilauea may be draining off enough magmatic pressure to keep them small. But a shift, a flexure of the crust on the ocean floor, and a new Mauna Kea, a new Diamond Head, may someday come steaming and smoking out of the sea.

Before that happens – if it happens – the island of Hawaii itself may be gone. It lies at the intersection of two enormous fractures, one that runs the length of the Hawaiian Ridge, the other a great rent in the earth called the Molokai Fracture. A modest mountain like Kaala on Oahu, only 4,040 feet high, exerts a pressure of twelve tons per square inch on its base. Mauna Loa and Mauna Kea are measured not in cubic yards but cubic miles of volume. The pressures they generate are not incalculable. But they are unthinkable. And Mauna Kea lies across those two fractures.

Hawaii trembles, more than any other island in the chain. Hardly formed, it is already on its way back into the sea. So, of course, is every island ever made, and for that matter every continent. But parts of Hawaii's coastline are sinking steadily at the rate of eight to twelve inches a century, three times as fast as is normal elsewhere in the world. Near Cape Kumukahi, the easternmost point of the island, the stumps of coconut trees that not long ago grew on a sandy beach now stand submerged even at low tide. On the west coast, the Kona coast, the earth shifts every so often along its fault lines, the ground level falls by several inches, or several feet, and large troughs appear. These are called grabens, or graves.

Anyone can see such things for himself. Yet the eye is not enough to tell us our true course.

Beneath the major islands the earth's crust is thick, far thicker than in the open ocean. This is the geologic stuff of which continents are made, and there is precedent for the elevation of islands. On the other hand, the volcanoes all along the chain may have an outburst left, in which – there is precedent for this too – the land will be reduced to fine red dust adrift in some apocalyptic sunset. In the vast, ancient, teeming, empty Pacific, anything is possible.

Man, of course, does not care to look extinction in the eye, and the breath of creation is suffocating. But in between is life, to be explained and ordered. The Hawaiians began, like everyone else, at the beginning, with a creation chant. Theirs was called the Kumulipo.

"At the time when the earth became hot
At the time when the heavens turned about
At the time when the sun was darkened
To cause the moon to shine
The time of the rise of the Makalii
The slime, this was the source of the earth
The source of the darkness that made darkness
The source of the night that made night
The intense darkness, the deep darkness
Darkness of the sun, darkness of the night
Nothing but night . . . "

Then (the Kumulipo is thousands of lines in length, and very little of creation goes unaccounted for), the coral is born, the sea urchin, the clam, the barnacle, the cowrie, the sea plants drifting in the shallows, the moss on the rocks, the ferns, the fish of the sea, the land animals, the useful plants of the forest, the indispensable taro. The tides ebb and flow, the mountains take shape, the sun shines, the stars turn in their courses. Man appears. Light replaces darkness. The world of nature is born.

Alone in his beautiful world for a thousand years, the Hawaiian learned to see and feel sensitively and intimately: the changes in cloud-shapes on a mountain, the perfect arch of a double rainbow across a valley, the serene procession of the waves, the shape and texture of shells, the grain of woods and stones, the shine of a single dewdrop on a leaf at dawn. His was an enchantment bred of familiarity. He loved all the things in nature that changed and yet stayed the same.

He matched his language to his vision, stringing polished words like smooth beads on long lines of melodic chant, so that he could keep with him at night the beauty that delighted him by day. So the Hawaiian was nursed on song. He was richly fed. The chants were pure, clear sound in an endless flow. Each time they were sung, beauty was liberated. And beyond

Carved Hawaiian god figures, City of Refuge,
Kona Coast, Island of Hawaii.

that, their poetry was powerful enough to shape and sustain the universe. The chanter delighted to describe the world we live in, and to evoke with the same words the meaning of other, hidden realms, the realms of the gods. The chant master, running his voice affectionately over the outlines of a beloved landscape, was really telling, again and again, the story of creation.

At Pearl Harbor before the war, Sam the Hawaiian riveter grinned and called me "blalah" for brother. Sam held the heavy, quivering hammer like a toy and his sweat danced on the redhot steel buttons. After work, his enormous hand enveloped a beer bottle so only the top was visible.

But Sam could not, or would not, tell me about being Hawaiian. Nor would Moses, a younger man who came from one of the last native families to live on Kahoolawe. Moses was tall and statue-handsome, but silent, withdrawn, wearing remoteness like a welder's helmet. He moved among us but not with us.

So I walked my curiosity about the town, back to the museum, into libraries. I talked to many people and read a great deal, wanting to know what the Hawaiian was like and how he lived before the white man came. It has turned into a strolling of many years and this is a summing of it:

Some 300,000 Hawaiians lived in the islands, moving in as near-perfect a balance with nature as man has attained.

Religion and law were one and above all were four great gods. Kane, the supremacy, was represented by the sun. Others were Lono, of fruitful earth; Ku, of power and force; and Kanaloa of the sea. All were males. Beneath them were dozens of lesser gods, some female: Pele of volcanoes, Hina of the moon, and Laka of dance. These are but a few. There were many thousands of other gods – of different rains,

winds, cliffs, lagoons, mountains and valleys. A fishpond acquired its own sacred spirit.

There were gods under gods under gods. Craftsmen, farmers, seers, midwives and meteorologists had occupational gods called akua. Tens of thousands of fishermen had their own gods, the kuula, enshrined in seashore altars. Lowliest, yet most personal of all, were the aumakua of a family. Some were carved in rude figures. Many were simple pieces of unworked coral or stone. Daily offerings of food and water were made and prayers chanted, not to the earth-scraps of the aumakua, but to their living power and protection.

Of the humans, only the alii, the high chiefs, conversed with the greater gods and communicated their benevolence – or rage. As descendants of the gods, this was their birthright. And through them the gods ruled.

This was the heathen, before the white man came.

Because nothing great or small in life escaped the attention of the gods, everything in life was subject to the kapu, the taboos. Because everything in life was charged in some way or another with divine power, it was dangerous, foolhardy, fatal in the end, to oppose the fields of force that played over the world. Kapu defined what might be joined, what kept apart, setting everything in proper relationship with everything else. It was the reason for doing things as they were done. Without it, life would have no shape, no order.

The life of the Hawaiians took its ultimate direction from the kapus. And so, in endless inventory, there were kapus for day and night, for the different months and seasons of the year, for ceremonies, occupations, pastimes. And for man alone, for man with the land and sea, for man with woman.

Great chiefs were born to the roll of thunder and the flash of lightning, the pounding of the surf, and the howl of winds bending the trees into submission. As children, they rode on the shoulders of attendants, so that their feet might not touch the ground. To keep their aristocratic blood undefiled, they married among themselves, and the highest of high marriages was between brother and sister. Bred and nourished for stature, the alii grew six-and-a-half feet tall and more, and the frame of a chief might carry a weight of 300 pounds. Robed in helmet and feather cloak, the alii filled the space between earth and sky, man and god.

"To the chief belongs the whole land;
To the chief belongs the ocean and the land;
The night is his; the day is his;
For him are the seasons – the winter, the summer,
The month, the seven stars of heaven now risen.
The property of the chiefs, above and below,
All things that float ashore, the bird driven upon
    the land;
The thick-shelled, broad-backed turtle, the dead
    whale is cut up;
The yearly Uhu of the sea.
Let the chief live forever! Evermore a chief!
Let him be borne forth gloriously with the short
    gods and the long gods.
Let him go forth fearlessly, the chief holding the
    island."

Their state temples were dedicated with human sacrifices, a man killed in the forest where the trees were felled, others buried beneath the corner posts. Their ceremonial lands were sacred. Commoners, to avoid casting a shadow on them, would take one trail past the boundary in the morning, another in the afternoon. No commoner could remain standing in the great man's presence; the wretch who failed to prostrate himself was fit only for death. The chiefs stood on the neck of their people. And for the most part the commoners bowed willingly, because the chief's own life guaranteed the life of all. When a high chief died, men and women tore out their hair and wailed and smashed their teeth and burned and gashed their bodies. The connections between god and man had been cut, and the world was whirling in black infinity.

But what was the ordinary Hawaiian like? What moved him? I would ask myself. And these are some of the answers:

Surely he knew lice, hunger, cold rain through thatch, occasional summons to war and other miseries. But he knew and lived these things too:

Life was a precious state and should be filled with beauty, joy and love, with courtesy and generosity. A stranger should not pass one's home without being invited to rest and eat. Unpleasant subjects were never discussed during a mealtime. All things were shared, even troubles. If one person was ill, or disturbed, his affliction was the concern of all. Hundreds of years before Freud or Jung, the ancients engaged in hooponopono, "making things right," the talking-out of problems. The family gathered and discussed the irksome matter freely, until solutions were found.

The aged and senile were cared for and there were no orphans. Childless couples were given children by others much blessed. And these hanai youngsters grew, knowing their ancestry but loving foster parents as their own.

Life began with birth and all births in nature were connected. Even stones took their shapes from sex. Leave a male

Left: Phallic Rock, near Kalae, Molokai.
Above: Female birthing stone, near Wahiawa, central Oahu.

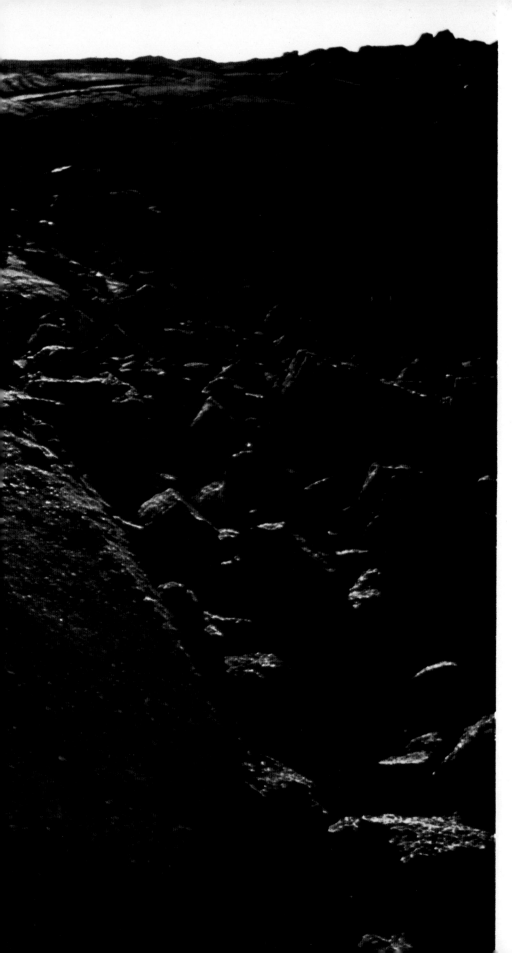

Petroglyph, Anaehoomalu, north Kona Coast,
Island of Hawaii.

and female stone together and there would be keikis, children. Water the infant stone and it would grow, perhaps into a god. One stony outcrop manifested more divine power than another – a good place for birthing a human child. So, take pain and joy to that place. And take the child, cut his umbilicus and free him for his own life. Then plant the piko, his navel string, secure and safe in a rock cavity, binding him again to the land and his ancestry. Carry him home at the nipple and strengthen him; mold his beauty with massaging, loving hands, croon a chanting to his fine forehead, well-defined nose, long straight limbs and shapely feet, sprinkle him with love. Bury him in sand and in struggling free, his muscles will gain power and form.

Watch him grow – big enough to carry a water gourd, a coconut, two coconuts, then a smaller child. Send him one day to live with men. Circumcise him, and place upon the scar a healing morning glory blossom. Sing his body's beauty to him. Name its handsome, virile parts. Teach him the loveliness of making beautiful children of his own.

This was the pagan, before the white man came.

Hawaiians, along with other Polynesians, have always impressed Westerners as the handsomest of people. The classical note has been sounded again and again, with due allowance made for a touch of less than classical portliness (put this down to poi). The fisherman on the rock, naked to his loincloth, must be a Greek statue in bronze; the girl surprised bathing in a waterfall (and Westerners surprised her so often she ceased to be surprised) could only be a naiad.

Constrained at last to wear nineteenth-century clothing, the men of Hawaii continued to carry themselves naturally, and the walk of the Hawaiian woman was a timeless triumph. "I never saw anything at all like it," wrote the sharp-eyed maiden-lady traveler Isabella Bird in the 1870s. "I should know a Hawaiian woman by it in any part of the world. A majestic wahine with small, bare feet, a grand, swinging, deliberate gait, hibiscus blossoms in her flowing hair, and a lei of yellow flowers . . . has a tragic grandeur of appearance, which makes the diminutive, fair-skinned haole, tottering along in high-heeled shoes, look grotesque by comparison." It was the walk of a female sure of her body.

The body was displayed at its best in the hula. One of Pele's sisters invented the dance, and it took its inspiration for movement from the trees and flowers and waves. Part obeisance to the gods but mostly entertainment, the hula ended often enough in the celebration of sex, which was what got it into trouble in the long run. The eighteenth century at least could look at it as art. Archibald Menzies, a Scottish surgeon accompanying an exploring expedition in the 1790s, was entertained on the slopes of Mauna Loa by an "opera girl." "Every joint of her limbs, every finger on her hand, every muscle of her body, partook unitedly of the varied sympathetic impulses, while the motion of her eyes transferring their transient glances and the harmony of her features were beyond the power of description."

Delightful; but the nineteenth century, which chose to withhold more from itself, could see only viciousness – or, worse still, nothing at all. The hula, as the Reverend Henry Cheever perceived it, "consisted merely of successive jumps with both feet at once, to a regular harsh sound from the lungs, and occasional slapping or drumming of the hands upon the bare breasts and sides, together with distortions of the countenance and gesticulations with the arms." A troupe went to the California gold fields, and the prediction in Christian circles at Honolulu was that their performances would be spurned as too obscene. The dancers failed, as being not *sufficiently* obscene. By the end of the century the confident performing body was at least covered with blouse, grass skirt – an innovation – and long underwear. Still the hula seemed to some a low and disgraceful affair, a thing that outsiders either should not see or should not want to see, and in the 1920s at Honolulu there occurred one of those splendid American trials at law in which the judge orders the offending dance done in the courtroom, to determine whether it is art or has, if nothing else, some redeeming social significance. The hula survived. Keep your eyes on the hands.

For me, times and feelings of the old ones are best savored in what they made and used – for living, for beauty and for the spirit – and above all the stones. The stones are a wonder.

Molten stone stirred the Hawaiians' earth. Stone was everywhere: stone of sensual porosity and textures; stone that begged handling and shaping; beach and stream stones, tumbled and buffed to millions of satin-smooth moldings. There was soft stone, cindery stone, stone tiny and immense. Stones for building, for shrines, trails, household gods, sinkers, anchors, slings of war and games of peace. Laboriously, bruisingly, the ancients chipped one against the other, forming precious adzes from densest basalt, quarried, sometimes in snow dustings, from the highest mountains, to be fashioned for farming, tree-felling, canoe and god-carving.

Just as slowly, patiently, they shaped other tools of coral, wood, bone and shell – objects of many uses and graceful forms. The making of these utensils, decorations or weapons took time, even weeks and months, but time brought the individual craftsman closer to his creation. Use made it part of him and infused it with his mana, his spirit, and it became an extension of himself and his soul.

From leaves of sedge and hala, pandanus, his women wove mats and cloths of linen-like suppleness. Paper mulberry bark they beat into the softest of tapa cloths. From the infinitesimal neck plumes of tiny birds they wove capes, shoulder cloaks and helmets of near-velvet softness; the few that still survive are precious museum pieces. Their thin, tough cordage of sennit compares with the strongest of our day; the fishhooks, bonito lures, anklets, necklaces and other ornaments were symmetrical achievements in bone, ivory and pearlshell.

The great heiaus, temples, were fashioned of hundreds of thousands of carefully placed stones. They stood, platforms of magnificence, in long ago suns – and many still stand, lost in thickets of today. Above them the god images, huge, fearsome carvings, once glared their challenges. Pahu, sharkskin drums, mounted on intricately carved human figures, once summoned the populace, and underscored priestly pronouncements. Treetrunk towers for oracles rose over altars for dedication, prayer and sacrifice presided over by the kahunas, the high and priestly caste.

The kahunas were the protectors, retainers, communicators of all the wisdoms of time and the gods. And over them, and over the alii and in everything were the gods – Kane, Lono, Ku and Kanaloa – the four gods, the forty, the forty thousand, the four hundred thousand gods.

This, I learned, was the heathen.

Life and their leaders taught the Hawaiians to treat land and sea with respect. They were without the wheel,

Shorebreak wave, Waimea Bay, windward Oahu.

beasts of burden, and metals. They were not earth-movers. They liked to feel their toes and fingers deep in the soil, taking hold on life. The water they loved. They swam and dived superbly, and invented surfing. They worked the reefs and played the waves, and salt spray was like holy water to them. They built their small thatched houses not far from the coast, as a rule, in sight of the ocean, in sight of the hills, so that each village could have timber from the forest and fish from the fecund sea.

Living plants and creatures too the Hawaiians treated with respect; after all, one of their greatest gods had stood on his head and turned himself into a breadfruit tree. Pigs might go snouting through the brush, tearing up the soil, and thatch-gatherers might set fire to grass one season so as to be sure of a sturdier crop the next, but the land and sea were never exploited to exhaustion. There were restrictions, set by calendar and custom. The kahuna would tie a piece of tapa cloth to coconut trees along the shore to show when fishing was prohibited. This was to give the tiny spawn time to grow for future food, and the seaweed time to replenish itself as food for fish and humans. Farmers knew that taro patches should be allowed to lie fallow a year or more at a time. And when a man went out looking for medicinal herbs he did so quietly and reverently, early in the morning, when nature was at her strongest, taking only what he needed, and giving thanks.

I chanced into Holani a long time ago while wandering the Big Island. No one asked my name or business. I was referred to simply as "The Haole."

Holani is a blessed oasis after a tortured landscape. Weatherworn houses with rusted corrugated roofing line the shore. There is the delicious cool green of shade again; palms nod lazily to each other, sharing secrets. The small and stony beach is scattered with canoes, vivid daubs in sunshine. Long gauzings of fishnets are stretched on poles pointing skyward, pennants to Holani's industry. Along the shore the volcano-river once boiled into the sea and tides pulse among dark and glistening stones.

I moved into a rickety shack at the far end of the village at the end of a shallow, sand-bottomed lagoon. Every day I fished along cliffs to a beach, where I stripped and had a long swim, drifting lazily in wine-water over black sand. My lunch was usually water from a canteen and cold beans from a can. Few meals have tasted better.

In the afternoons I idled back to the village and took my catch to the storekeeper. He selected the best kinds and tossed others aside almost apologetically. He weighed the small pile, then ceremoniously opened a big ledger. My account occupied a page titled "The Haole" and he toted up the value of the offering and recorded it in a large schoolboy hand. He gave me canned goods, tobacco, matches and other things in return. There was never mention of money. Often he complimented me on the catch and I'm certain it was done in kindness.

He was a quiet and shy man and is now dead. He is one of the few men I ever truly enjoyed doing business with. His name is on a gravestone, lost somewhere on the Mauna Loa mountainside. Permit me to record it here. Hulama.

The land set its own limits, but they were generous. Most important was the flow of water, because life flowed with it. The great god Kane was the life force, and never more powerful than as Kaneikawaiola, Kane-in-the-waters-of-life. Wealth for the Hawaiians was waiwai, water doubled and intensified, and the word for law was kanawai, things having to do with water, the regulation of water.

The irrigated taro patches, terraced and banked and ditched, took their shape from the flow of water in the valleys, and the making of a new terrace, a new addition to life and wealth under the law, began with the treading of the earth floor. "It was a festival day," wrote the native historian Samuel Manaiakalani Kamakau. "Pig and fish and vegetables were laid in to refresh the treaders. Every man, woman and child decked himself with leaves and worked with all his might, tramping here and there, stirring the mud with his feet, dancing, rejoicing, reveling and indulging in all kinds of sport. This was done so that the water would not sink into the soil, and allow the taro to grow."

Cooked, pounded, kneaded with water, taro becomes poi, the authentic Hawaiian delight. The Hawaiian ate poi constantly, grew big and fleshy and strong on it, talked about it, argued about it, made up stories about it. He was a connoisseur of age and taste and variety. No winesman's palate was ever more delicate in its discriminations.

The gentle observances of a devoted, elderly poi eater are infatuated, specific, endless. Never talk business around the poi bowl. Never refuse a stranger a place. Wash the hands before and after eating. Use one or two or three fingers according to the consistency of the poi. Dip them to about the first joint. Never pull the hand roughly through poi. Rotate the fingers gently, withdraw them mildly, wave the hand, while conversation goes on, gracefully back and forth to keep the poi from falling until the mouth is ready for swallowing. Then eat, smacking the lips politely. Never comment on how much others take. When everyone has finished, clean the bowl with the fingers.

And give eternal thanks, in word and deed, for the blessing of poi. There never was a Hawaiian who did not like it. In the old days, poi *ruled*. Hereditary chiefs were called kalokanuokaaina, taro-planted-in-the-land, and as late as the 1880s a civilized Hawaiian king, whose genealogical chants showed him to be descended from the first taro plant, had the taro designed into his crown. Poi, poi, poi: what other food could there be so wise, modest, heroic, replete with virtue?

A consuming attachment, and more than digestive – mystical, in fact, and desperately important to the Hawaiians. A family group was called ohana, and this word came from oha, which meant the sprouts on a taro corm (itself called makua – parent or father). A family's land was called aina, from ai, meaning feeding or food, and referring specifically to poi. Oha, ai, aina, ohana – taro sprouts, food, the land, the family: they were inseparable.

Each man's life wound its way across the fruitful land and seascape. The gods had decided that all days should be much the same length, and they did not mark the seasons distinctly. Still, there were signs to help men follow the year through, on the land, in the sea, in the sky. The moon waxed and waned, the sun made its long journey south and back, the familiar constellations advanced to array themselves above the islands and withdrew again. The winds shifted back and forth, migrating birds came and went, the mullet spawned and then the flying fish, the plume of the sugarcane unsheathed itself.

Left: Taro plants, Waipio Valley, Island of Hawaii.
Below: Planting young taro, Waipio Valley.

In Holani the days genuflect to one another. They are days of peace and warmth, of grace and gentle occupation. There are no noises, only music – the whisper of the tide pool, the gossip of coconut trees, the laughter and splashing of children.

Waking in the morning I could see an old woman in the lagoon, a squat, dark figure on glass-still water, standing up to her knees, circles rippling out when she moved. She fished for ohua, the fingernail-size striped baby manini. In one hand she carried a palm frond and in the other a scoop net. The tiny fish traveled in schools and the palm frond served as an aquatic broom. She swept the fish into the net with slow, sure motions. When she had a small pailful of the glistening creatures she went ashore on some lava rocks that formed a little island. A flat space of boards was rigged atop some poles and she spread the fish out on it. They flapped and danced and she placed them under a wire screen for drying. The ohua were delicious eating, crisp and tasty. Through the day I carried a pocketful like so much small change, popping them in my mouth like peanuts . . .

In late afternoon the canoes came home. Women of the village appeared casually from quiet shacks and strolled to the crescent inlet. A few helped arrange thin round poles on the shore, then many dragged the craft over rollers to a high and safe place. Two fishermen emptied the canoe of nets, buckets, jugs and lines; one woman took a can and bailed water from the lower end. All were silent until someone ventured the question: "Get?"

And a man answered, "Get plenty."

He lifted the board-decking of a center well and the villagers peered in, muttering approbation. The coffin-shaped recess was packed with the still-shuddering, bright-eyed harvest from beyond the reef. The glittering wet mass contained silvery opelu mackerel, big-eyed scad, elliptic pom-pano, red-banded goatfish, striped manini and rainbowed parrotfish.

The women took turns reaching into the canoe and plucking out what was desired. The men, busy with cleanup chores, paid no attention. There was no asking, no thanking. The fish were there and plentiful and for everyone. To-morrow, someone else would have fish. If anyone had need he would be welcome. It has always been this way, this sharing, this aloha. And the women walked slowly back to their homes, clutching the tails of supper . . .

After the sun sets, its warmth lingers for a long time on the earth. Walking barefoot is a little memory of the day. The twilight creatures appear. Mottled crabs scamper over the beach, their eyes perched on twitching antenna. They chase leaves and scraps of waste, their quick stiff claws testing, tasting, and rejecting. When a dog or wandering mongoose roams near, they vanish in a finger-snap. A wave rinses the beach, the foam recedes and only bursting bubbles mark their dungeons. A yellow-eyed cat sends black crabs into panicky flight over boulders. Sea birds dip and flutter along the line of surf, going home.

A soothing wind drifts from the mountain and cools the lava waste. Its fingers reach into the village and stir the palms, explore the shacks and stone fences and signal the lighting of coconut-husk and charcoal fires. The smoke-incense rises, the night-perfume of Holani. Kerosene lan-terns glow on the creaky lanais, radiating golden circles of family and friendship.

After supper the children are rolled in blankets and put to rest, "Moemoe mo'opuna," the women whisper, "sleep, sleep, little one." Calloused, scarred hands tenderly tuck covers and turn to other tasks. In dim light they mend nets, unsnarl lines and roll final cigarettes. There is soft talk of the

day and the day to come and the age-old greeting: "Hele mai!
Nou ka hale! – Come in! The house is yours!"
And night comes like a benediction to Holani.

At the turn of each year came a festival celebrating fruitfulness. This was the makahiki, and its special god was Lono, whose priests prayed to him for rain and abundant crops. Commoners kept a food gourd filled with Lono in mind, and the pious prayed over it each day, morning and evening, and ate some of the god's food for him. The earth itself was Lono's food gourd. He filled it every year to overflowing, and for this the Hawaiians thanked him. A profuse thanks: on some of the islands the makahiki festival lasted four months.

It was the happiest of times. War was outlawed, criminals might be pardoned. Serious occupations were suspended, and the hula flourished. There were games and sporting contests to watch, and feasts to enjoy. Lono made his appearance on the coast, represented by an image like a mast and sail made of wood and tapa cloth, decorated with ferns and feather leis and anointed with coconut oil. In procession he made his way around each island, greeted at every stopping point by joyful crowds. The hula dancers followed in their green and flowery finery, and the boxers, wrestlers, and runners strained their strength.

The Hawaiians had the greatest of talents for good-humored public performance, and the makahiki was their high season for this, month after month of it. It is another of those Hawaiian appetites that has fed on itself, and somehow there has always been enough to go round. Everyone in the islands has eaten from Lono's food gourd. He has been gone now for the better part of two centuries but the appetite for holidaying is stronger than ever, and the modern calendar reads like one long festival chant.

There was another point to the makahiki, masked but not obscured in the festivities. It was tax time. Gifts for the gods, and for the chiefs too: pigs, fish, taro, bananas, breadfruit, tapa cloth, woven mats, carved wood, and feathers for the red and yellow royal cloaks. All this wealth the chief took by right.

But after the festival of Lono came the ceremonies of Ku, the war god, and each of the islands had great chiefs ready to take the good things given by the gods of fertility and turn them to the purposes of Ku.

The gods of fertility had been kind, to the point where they had to cease to be kind. Fertility in humans had to defer to the limits of the land. The gods taught the priests how to regulate the supply of food with kapus, reserving the best for chiefs and for men in general, denying the women. The women learned how to end unwanted life as it began, with abortion and infanticide.

The alii never did learn self-denial. There were many high chiefs, and each somehow heard the gods say he had it in him to be all-powerful. Someday, then, one man would bestride all the islands, blotting out with his feather cloak the sun of his enemies' lives.

The chiefs waged war as fiercely as they knew how. The gods taught them ambition and lust for power, yet somehow withheld the means of efficient destruction. There was iron in the Hawaiian earth, but it remained hidden, and war was fought with wood and stone. It was the white man who knew best about war. It was his coming that drove the iron into the soul.

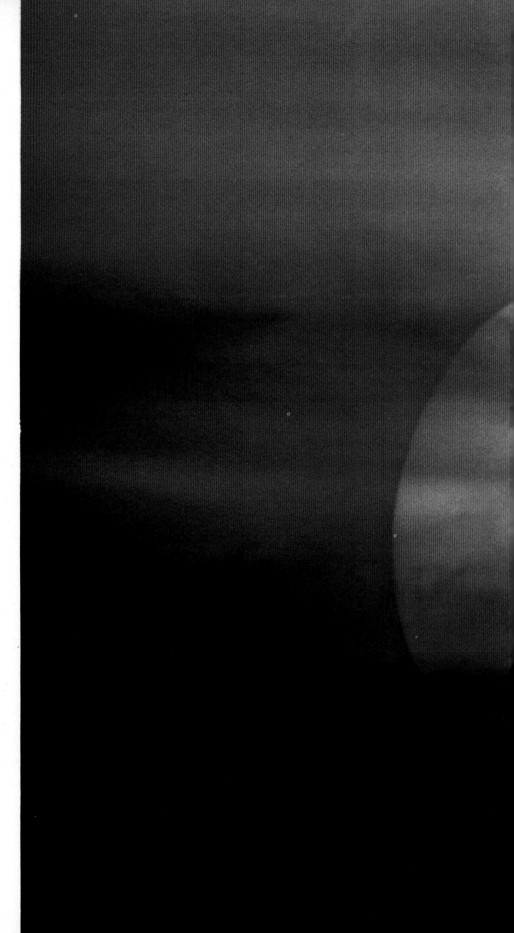

Right: Winter sunset, Waikiki Beach, Oahu.

III Discoveries

James Cook was an officer of the British Navy and a great man. His work was exploring, his field of operations the Pacific, and his special gift was making unprecedented discoveries, one after the other, systematically, until no one in Europe could be left in doubt about his genius.

In the eighteenth century, when travel was one of the addictions of armchair intellectuals, Cook's expeditions were great openers of the mind. His first two voyages to the South Pacific spanned several years, covered a quarter of the globe, and brought the existence of Polynesia to the attention of the world. His third was to take him into the Pacific north of the equator, to look for something that Europeans had not been able to find in three hundred years of searching: the Northwest Passage, a track across the frozen seas above the American continent.

Cook did not find the Northwest Passage. It was not there to be found, at least not by the ships he had – the *Resolution* and the *Discovery*. They were the sort of vessel he had grown up with and used by preference, converted coal-haulers, small, bluff-bowed, very maneuverable on winding coasts and around the convoluted shores of islands – sturdy, seaworthy, but no twentieth-century icebreakers. Instead, on his way north from the Society Islands to the northwest coast of America, Cook found the Hawaiian archipelago. It was the last of his oceanic discoveries, and, he judged, in many ways the most important.

Cook himself is not easy to discover. His professional life is in his logs and journals, a record of sharp-eyed observation and intelligent speculation. About himself there is practically nothing. He was not given to written introspection. He seems to have been almost without private life. He had emotions: he was capable of rage, but mostly against technical incompetence whenever it turned up on his ships. More than anything else, he cared about his work, and here he was almost obsessive. He had, he said, "Ambition not only to go further than anyone had done before, but as far as it was possible for man to go." And he meant to know where he had been, and to make a rational record of it. He had an infinite passion, then, for exactitude – not of the finicky pathological kind, but a passion for the measurable dimensions of reality. A very Western passion, almost a religion.

Aboard the *Resolution* and the *Discovery* on Cook's third voyage, the object of this passion was a recent invention, a silver watch about five inches in diameter – a marine chronometer, capable of keeping exact time. It was a British piece of work. Only a few had been made, and Cook of course was the best man to make use of one. The chronometer was capable of reducing the flux of time at sea to identical measured fragments, and this meant that a navigator could calculate distances between any two points, east and west, on earth.

For more than two centuries, white men had blundered about the Pacific, able to make reasonably accurate calculations for latitude, but reduced essentially to hoping for the best about longitude. With the chronometer, though, time acquired a habitation, at the Royal Observatory at Greenwich, near London, the point of origin of an expanding Western civilization. Time started there, distance began there. The circling degrees of longitude led always home again.

Cook's chronometer – "our never failing guide the

Watch," "our trusty friend the Watch" – was enshrined in a safe box guarded by three good locks with different wards. The captain held one key, the first lieutenant another, a professional astronomer the third. Each day at noon the watch was wound in their presence. The time was correlated with readings taken from celestial bodies. Figures were recorded and attested by the observers, and then the watch was locked away for twenty-four hours. The daily ritual held the explorer's world together and gave it order. The chronometer was a kind of scientist's god.

Cook, half a world away from Greenwich, came upon the Hawaiian Islands at daybreak on January 18, 1778. By then he and his men were old hands at this matter of the tropic landfall – the mountains coming up out of the sea soft and blue and indistinct in the dawn, the surf breaking white on the reef close in, the sun warm on a sweep of sand. Beauty in Polynesia was taken for granted; it was not written about any more. Surprise at the existence of these most isolated islands in the world was small; after years at sea in the Pacific, Cook was a hard man to surprise.

The islands appeared one by one, from northeast to north to northwest, until there were three – Oahu, Kauai, Niihau. Natives came out in canoes to stare up at the decks; white men looked down over the ships' rails. Gifts were exchanged, words were spoken. Connections were made – small discoveries, part of a greater one.

The navigational readings were taken, the log was written up. Hawaii was real for Cook now, attached to the West by uncuttable lines of great skill, inventiveness, and practical calculation.

I know about myself and why I troll for marlin. It is a rite, a chosen boredom that can be electrified by intense excitement; a catnap bursting into pandemonium with the strike; the taste of cold beer from bottles; deliciousness of slapped-together sandwiches; conquest, many things.

But often, I have wondered about the great fish, and how his hours may flow before the encounter . . .

Perhaps he lazes slowly, full-fed and fathoms deep where it is dark and cold. Above is the bluish surface glow. On one side coral shoulders slope off the reef-shelf. On the other is the endless, bottomless black . . .

Or possibly, he has spent hours hunting tuna with a porpoise school. As an outsider, he would have to work the fringes of their feeding, careful not to offend the mammals, knowing death can be dealt from blows of their iron-bottle snouts. So he may not have eaten well and veered to hunt alone, gulping vagrant bonito . . .

Instinctively, he heads west, closer to the lee side of the island where luck has always been better. His gelatinous, teacup-size eyes are on constant scan. Feeding and survival are fulltime occupations in his world. He moves slowly but purposefully, rising now and then to the surface, his dorsal beating air and his long snout flicking skyward, as if sniffing. He must sense that flying fish and small tuna feel his nearness, that they panic and scatter like flung coins. But surely he is not aware that he is a creature of massive power, a ponderous poem of blues and silver.

And the fish could know nothing about me, a mile away, lolling in the fighting chair of the charter boat. As a frigate bird soars high above, following the shadowed form, knowing it leads to food, I can look inshore at the cool blue monuments of the Waianae Range. And think of a time when I watched a big silver marlin poised in a long leap across the

68

Below: Stone altar to fish god Kunihi,
Kaunolu, Lanai.
Right: Frigate bird in evening sky,
North Kona Coast, Island of Hawaii.

canyon between two great waves. And of how he hung, suspended and glistening for a moment, the wildest, loveliest, most noble creature I had ever seen.

The crewman packs more beer on ice, tucking it tenderly, as if he were putting little babies to bed. The skipper stands forward on the glowing mahogany floor of the deckhouse. The boat is a fine, rich craft, sleek, chromed, shining with pride. The tackle is the best and the big reels gleam. Back in white water churned by the screws, baits leap and tumble, then plunge under the surface, trailing cottony wake-strings. The rods arc and shudder under the tuggings. Outriggers dip toward the water as we roll and plow ahead.

Perhaps, I tell myself, this is the day. I have been waiting a long time. Everything is prepared for a meeting. But it is being arranged by chance.

Will he be twice – three – four times my weight?

Perhaps, even now, we are on paths that will cross in half an hour. When we do, our worlds will explode.

And the marlin will lose.

Cook was a consummate technician, but more than that. He had a care for people – his crew, most of whom would have signed to sail with him anywhere, and Polynesians too. He had discovered them, and so felt responsible for them in a way. By and large he liked them, and in his inquiring, reasonable fashion found their society interesting and worth thinking about. He did not find them flawless. It was European intellectuals who *invented* the Polynesian, and that was a different matter altogether.

They did it out of Cook's work. The journals of his voyages were published one after another. Cook was no literary man – he was the son of a farm laborer and

his prose was not considered graceful enough to go unadorned before the educated public. So he was edited for sophistication. The journals – like the voyages themselves – were great successes. The islands were displayed like beautiful maps of reason and sensibility, and the Polynesian became the philosophic marvel of the age, the Noble Savage.

Everybody talked about Noble Savages. Very few people saw one. Joseph Banks, the naturalist who went with Cook on his first voyage, proposed to have a Polynesian brought home: "I do not know why I may not keep him as a curiosity, as well as some of my neighbours do lions and tygers . . ." One indeed came to London with Cook's second expedition. The curiosity, a Society Islander named Omai, was instantly lionized: interrogated by scholars, painted by portraitists, rhapsodized over by poets, ogled by titled beauties. The unstoppable conversationalist Samuel Johnson, at first not impressed, brought himself to concede that a savage might at least learn something from a sojourn among genteel Englishmen. But Johnson insisted (as was his habit) on having the last word. No savage, he thought, could be utterly noble. Human nature was everywhere a mixture of virtue and vice; "the Creator doth not appear partial in his distributions."

No one had seen more of the Creator's distributions than Cook, and the idea of the Noble Savage was distinctly not his: it was read into him. The Polynesian had a brief and spectacular vogue, then fell abruptly from fashion, for the simplest of reasons – he was not as advertised. Omai might learn to hold a fork and a conversation, but what did that signify? In the Marquesas, the Noble Savage was a cannibal. The proud

Carved god figures, City of Refuge,
Island of Hawaii.

Kukailimoku, war god of Kamehameha the Great,
Bishop Museum, Honolulu.

New Zealand warrior was also an opportunistic dealer in human heads, and when in the nineteenth century supplies ran short, he would turn a man into trade goods on the spot rather than lose a sale. The life-loving Tahitian practiced abortion, infanticide, and human sacrifice. And the affable, welcoming Hawaiian – the Hawaiian killed Cook.

It was easy for brown men and white men, whether in Europe or in the Pacific, to be confused about each other, looking only for what they wanted to see. Londoners thought Omai was noble; Hawaiians took their white discoverer to be divine.

Cook's expedition touched twice at the islands, the first time in January, 1778, at Kauai and Niihau toward the western end of the chain, and a year later farther east, at Kealakekua Bay on the island of Hawaii. Both times the natives were in the middle of their annual makahiki festival. The Hawaiians were enraptured by his ships that looked like floating forests and his men with their baggy blue and white "skins" and heads horned like the crescent moon. They concluded that Cook was their own god of fertility, Lono, coming from the sea to bless the traditional celebrations held in his honor.

For more than two weeks at Kealakekua the Englishmen were feted. The whole district heaped food and gifts on them. Crowds followed wherever they went. Women sang and danced for their delight, and competed to spend the night aboard ship. For Cook, nothing was too good. The great chief of the island exchanged names with him and gave him feather cloaks. The priests of Lono honored him with their most sacred rituals, and allowed him to set up his astronomical observatory on a temple platform. The chronometer was measuring eternity.

Cook was in command of the situation, as he always was. That was his business. He could have asked for and got anything he wanted from the Hawaiians. After two weeks, he had all the food and stores he needed. His men were rested, not to say sated with the hospitality of the Hawaiians. Cook had no more use for Kealakekua. There was work to be done elsewhere – the other islands of the chain to be explored and mapped, then another season in the Arctic to be organized.

Cook made his decision to leave Kealakekua just as the makahiki was coming to an end. He sailed away, just as the departing god Lono always did.

Silent, in thin cold air, high above the ranch country, the guide motioned us to stop.

The dozen wild sheep below were tiny from the height, heads down, nibbling at sparse brown patches. We started down and it was a long time before the guide turned, finger at his lips, crouched and pointing. We crept, then, a painful, muscle-tugging crawl through thickets that clawed, scratched and snared. Then the wait, squatting in silence, staring at a clearing the animals would have to cross.

Suddenly, they came – a bursting of shaggy forms, panicked as the wind turned and they scented man. Their flying file leapt across the narrow lane of vision. Guns roared and ripped at the ear.

The ram was dead when we got to him, eyes wet-dull, his coarse coat matted with dust, his heavy body limp and warm. The cowboy-guide hacked off the hind quarters and plunged his knife into the groin. "Mountain oysters," he smiled, holding up the limp bag of testicles. "Damn good, roasted."

Then there was the long climb up and back down again through arid brush, boots crackling and sliding over slaggy lava waste. At 7,000 feet on the volcano flank we breathed in gulps. Resting, the perspiration cold under loose jackets, we shuddered. At the end of it, at the jeep with cups of coffee laced with whiskey, someone remembered the mountain oysters, forgotten far up the mountainside.

"Want to go back and get them?" the guide asked. We looked back up at the miles of tortuous trail, shrouded now in a gathering mist.

"Not even if they were mine," one of us said.

Cook had to go back to Kealakekua. His ship, the *Resolution*, with a damaged mast, needed repairs. This was lost time, and something else was happening to time that the chronometer did not indicate. Once the makahiki was over for the Hawaiians, time did not belong any more to Lono, but to Ku, the god of war.

Lono never came back twice. Cook did. So, seen the second time, he might or might not be Lono. God or not, though, he still had something the Hawaiians could not get enough of – iron. Already they had traded everything they could in the way of food and women for pieces of metal to be hammered into tools and weapons.

On the night of February 13, 1779, they stole a cutter from the *Resolution's* sister ship, the *Discovery*, to burn it for its metal fittings. Cook went ashore next morning with a handful of marines. He was going to take the great chief hostage and keep him until the stolen boat was brought back. Cook did not believe in using his guns unnecessarily. Usually he got what he wanted with hostages – at least he had in the South Pacific.

This time things were different. Cook was threatening a ruling chief at the very moment when warriors, men of Ku, the war god, were ritually bound to protect their ruler. A crowd gathered on the beach to watch Cook walking the chief down to the boat. There was some opposition, and a scuffle. The marines fired. Cook, defending himself, killed a man with a musket shot, and in seconds he was cut down himself, stabbed and clubbed to death at the water's edge.

The Englishmen could hardly comprehend the disaster, and the Hawaiians themselves did not quite understand what their warriors had done. Lono's priests dismembered Cook's body, as though he were a chief worthy of deification, or indeed a god in human form. They gave some of the flesh and bones to the Englishmen, to be buried in the bay, asking at the same time whether Lono was angry, and when he would come again. And for years afterward they carried the rest of Cook's bones with Lono's tapa banners in the makahiki procession.

Among the watchers on the shore when Cook came to Kealakekua Bay was a young chief named Kamehameha. He saw what everybody else saw, made swift sense out of the sound of gunfire, and used his perceptions to become king of the islands.

Kamehameha was no fashionable Noble Savage. He was tall and strong and intelligent, but he did not have the looks for it otherwise. He stared, a young and unruly chief, out of "as savage a looking face" as Cook's men ever saw. One of the Englishmen thought he made a "clownish and blackguard appearance." Looks deceive.

Within three years of Cook's death Kamehameha

Petroglyph men going off to war, burial cave,
Keahole, Island of Hawaii.

Above: Olomana Peak, late evening, windward Oahu.

Right: Hawaiian burial cave, South Kona Coast,
Island of Hawaii.

was on his way to power on the island of Hawaii. A few more years, and he had a small Western ship and a cannon. He built up a mixed army of musketeers and spearsmen, the biggest fighting force the islands ever saw before the United States Army arrived at the end of the nineteenth century. His navy of schooners and decked canoes made a flotilla a mile long as he went conquering. He became an absolute ruler, something the islands had not had before.

It has been usual to call Kamehameha the Napoleon of the Pacific. This is unfair to Kamehameha. He neither led an insane march on Moscow nor suffered a Waterloo, and he killed only by the score, not by the hundred thousand. The Battle of Nuuanu, which gave him control of the major islands, cost the lives of only a few hundred men, caught and cut down at the head of a valley near Honolulu, or forced in desperation to jump to their deaths from a cliff, at whose base bones are still turned up every so often. It is an impressive spot, the Nuuanu Pali, with high winds gusting and razorback ridges cutting at the skyline and the cliff face falling away a thousand feet.

Cannon won the Battle of Nuuanu for Kamehameha. He collected big guns, and white men to fire them. He had a passion for ships to carry his warriors from island to island, and for silver dollars to buy more ships and guns. His plan was to amass so much power that he would never have to use any of it. He succeeded.

Power corrupted neither his looks nor his character. His "riper years," said an Englishman who knew him well, "softened the stern ferocity which his younger days had exhibited, and . . . changed his general deportment to an address characteristic of an open, cheerful and sensible mind; combined with great generosity, and goodness of disposition."

Kamehameha had no intention of letting power slip into the hands of the foreigner, the haole. Ships in the new Pacific and China trade – furs from the northwest coast of America, sandalwood from the islands – followed the explorers to Hawaii. But no merchantman put in without Kamehameha's knowledge; no trade was carried on without his permission. The price of a sojourn at Hawaii was high, and remarks about the naivete of natives grew scarcer in merchant captains' journals after Kamehameha came to his kingdom. Gifts of dress uniforms, brought by naval commanders with salutations from kings and czars, were acknowledged for what they were worth. "The uniforms which King George wears shine very much," said Kamehameha judiciously, "but can be of no service to me, because Kamehameha outshines everything." Even the haole god. Let a religious Westerner jump from a cliff and have his God save him; then Kamehameha would decide for himself what Christianity was worth.

You can see them from almost anywhere in the islands, the iwa, the frigate birds, sailing home at dusk. They pause and float over the town, harbors, quiet beaches – as if reluctant to leave the sea.

And when I see them I must pause too, for they enrapture with a grace disguising banditry. Against an orange sky of twilight they are sharp, ominous ink-scratches, thin, hard creatures with long-boned wings and forked tails.

For long days they sail under searing sun over far waters, hooked beaks dipped, yellow eyes staring. They watch for

Overleaf: Hawaiian hand-made lava saltpan
during rainstorm, Keahole, Island of Hawaii.

83

*the flying malolo, the darting tuna, diving to snatch them
from above wave tops. And when this fails they are bullies
and robbers, cruelly tearing the food from other sea birds.*

*But they are a loveliness, going home – hovering in a
slowmotion ballet, a reversed retribution. They return to
nestings high on mountainsides to feed their screeching
young and to rest.*

*All through the days their talons do not touch water. For
if they do, the birds cannot escape, and will die.*

Hawaii had never had a king before Kamehameha, just
chiefs in competition; and this was true of the rest of
Polynesia as well. Hawaiian history has always been
short of heroes, genuinely great men as opposed to
mere civic dignitaries. Cook and Kamehameha, the
discoverer and the unifier, are the only two for the
better part of a hundred years. They make an instructive
pair. The white man with a reasonable view of brown
men, the brown man with a utilitarian view of white
men; the civilized man whose forbearance about guns
probably cost him his life, the primitive who saw at
once that guns were everything, and came to power
with cannons and muskets – and never used them again.

Cook spoke almost never of himself and just once of
his ambitions. His maps are his true memorial.

Kamehameha was another man who said little and
did much. He died in 1819, forty years after Cook, and
there is no pilgrimage to be made to his grave. He lies
somewhere in secret on the island of Hawaii: "the
morning star alone knows where Kamehameha's bones
are guarded."

He does have a statue, though, a polychrome delight
commissioned for the centenary of Cook's discovery,
sculpted in Italy, and unveiled in 1883 opposite Iolani
Palace in Honolulu, home of the later monarchs. The
gilt feather cloak, helmet and loincloth are fine and
flamboyant, the bronze legs splendidly muscular. But
the stance of the statue was copied, evidently, from a
Roman piece – the emperor Augustus haranguing his
soldiers. Certainly the gesture – arm outstretched, palm
up, hand loosely open – is most un-Hawaiian. When,
recently, the Visitors Bureau wanted to use the outline
of the figure as a guidepost for tourist sights, the
guardians of authenticity complained. A chief would
never point. Now the roadside emblems have their
arms folded.

On Kamehameha Day each year, a public holiday,
the statue is heaped with flower leis. And there are any
number of Hawaiians who will, after a drink or two,
proudly claim descent from Kamehameha. It is a
powerful identification. There was never a greater
Hawaiian, or one better able to hold his own in a
difficult world. His name means The Lonely One.

Captain Cook has a modest monument at Kealakekua
Bay, just an obelisk, and tourist boats come down
almost every day now from the new hotels along the
coast. It used to be possible to find trees along the beach
splintered by gunfire in 1779. Now the native vege-
tation is crowded by foreign transplants. Earth
tremors and tidal waves have altered the shoreline.

The tourist boats nudge their way into the shallows.
The anchors go out, automobile engine blocks on the
end of a rope. People sit, waiting for the diver to bring
them up a souvenir sea urchin. If it is a hot day they will
drink a soda and drop the can in the water, and watch
it winking metallically down on the coral bottom.

IV   Tides

By the time Kamehameha the Great died in 1819, there were not many Hawaiians alive who knew what the world had been like before Cook. Where the haole came from and what he really wanted – these things were not clear. But it was obvious that the Hawaiian gods had not much to say about the comings and goings of foreigners. The haole did not respect the kapu days of gods, the kapu grounds of chiefs. And he did not seem to suffer for it. He was rich, powerful, the possessor of magic the Hawaiian could hardly begin to comprehend: metal-working, gunpowder, circum-navigation, writing. He was no god, but he could do things that made the Hawaiian gods look small.

The idea that man can snap his fingers at the gods has a horrible fascination. The haole, just by the fact of his existence, led the Hawaiian to try it. The haole seemed a free man; the Hawaiian came to think of himself as prisoner of the kapus. The chains began to chafe.

As long as Kamehameha was alive, things changed only as he allowed them to. He commanded gods and haoles both – a great man. That he was great and that he was a man – both were important after his death. His son and heir, Liholiho, was less of a man. And Kamehameha, with a score of wives to match his powers and his passions, left some formidable widows.

For female chiefs, the kapus were especially confining. They enjoyed the privileges of their rank and paid the penalties of their sex. The loftiest, with the power of life and death over commoners, could not even eat a meal with their men. Every day, every week, every month, they were reminded that the kapus cursed them with inferiority.

It was the women who challenged the gods.

Keopuolani was the mother of the new king. Kaahumanu was the favorite wife of the old king; full-fleshed, robust, imperious, uncontrollable, a natural force. These two were Eves of great appetite. They wanted the experience and the knowledge of god-baiting. They did not offer an apple in secret. They set a feast of foods forbidden to women, and called the king to eat with them, in public.

Liholiho could hardly tell whether this was a feast of death or a feast of life, whether the earth would open and swallow everyone, or merely shift and give the Hawaiians a new, secure place to stand. He went back and forth, back and forth, oppressed by the weight of the past, appalled at the void of the future. Then at last he ate. And killed the gods.

The temples did not heave; the graves did not open; the islands did not sink into the sea. A few traditionalists protested. They were put to flight with the guns so sensibly amassed by Kamehameha. So it was not so much after all – a meal, the rout of some malcontents. Yet the Hawaiians had done something so singular that there does not seem to be a parallel anywhere in the uncivilized world. They had given up their religion in favor of nothing, nothing at all. And so they went on into the nineteenth century, without divinity to sustain them, haunted at every turn by ghosts from the past and omens of alienation.

In a far village on the Big Island there is an old Hawaiian named Martin. Through the years and because of my love of fishing and camping, we have become friends and he has told me, in fragments, many things. He is old now, hard and thin and the ocean is a part of him. He feels its moods, knows its caprices, is completely at one with it. When Martin was a child, thousands of his people still lived in the settlements along the coast. But that was fifty years ago and now he is alone with the ghosts.

Sometimes, late in the night, with clouds scudding over crisp stars, he feels the old days, sees the fires on the beaches and hears the ancient chants. Many times he has been awakened by the tramping feet of the Night Marchers. The sounds of the spirit-column are far away at first, then they slowly mount as the marchers near. The fear in Martin rises and he strips himself, as was done in past days, and lies face down on the lava so the ghosts will not see him and be disturbed by his presence. Martin told me sometimes the marchers walk in the air just above the ground but the scraping of their feet on the cindered lava is loud and harsh.

A few times Martin has dared to look at the marchers. There are many hundreds – great dark soldiers carrying spears, the kahuna priests in their white wrappings of tapa cloth, the lesser chiefs and retainers wearing gold feather shoulder capes that gleam dully in moonlight, and the kahili bearers, holding high the feathered plumes of royalty.

But when the manele, the man-borne carriage of the highest chief of all approaches, Martin quickly turns his face again into the stones. For to look upon the alii-ai-moku is to invite instant death from the clubs of the king's guard.

In later years, Martin tells me, the marchers have not appeared as frequently. I suspect the ghosts still visit but they only look at the old man and smile. He harms no one, and soon he will be among them.

One other creature of the spirit – the Noble Savage – ought to have fallen with the kapus and died with the gods, killed at long last by experience. Yet he refused to die. Civilized men willed him to go on living because they needed him. The latecomer searching for the Savage was really on a journey to the interior. His destination was an island of the mind, and it would be his good fortune to find a Noble Savage in himself.

But most voyages to the islands after Kamehameha's death were made by another kind of men, nineteenth-century "improvers" of one sort or another, men certain of themselves, bringing demonstration kits of a better world. The program had begun with Cook.

"Being desirous of helping these poor people," Cook left the Hawaiians goats and pigs. George Vancouver left cattle, and Kamehameha put a kapu on them so they could breed and become established. Richard Cleveland brought horses from California in 1803. The rest of the Western menagerie followed, chewing its way remorselessly from the seashore to the highlands.

Cattle got to the top of Manoa valley behind Honolulu and came back down again to nibble the house gardens of the town. The natives were set to work in 1831 building a six-foot fence to keep them out. The beasts blighted the uplands of East Maui. They ran wild in scores of thousands on the slopes of Mauna Kea until well into this century, and now there are square miles of useless country where the grass is gone and the topsoil is washed away. The wild sheep stand on their hind legs and stretch their necks to get at the leaves of the mamane tree.

On the small island of Kahoolawe, off Maui, all the cover was long ago eaten and the soil pounded into dust by the hooves of goats. The water has dried up, no men have lived there for years, and the Navy uses the place for a bombing range. Shell-shocked goats

Torchfishing, first light,
Kaneohe Bay, windward Oahu.

Above: Net fishing for moi at dawn, near Makena,
southeast coast of Maui.
Right: Catching opai for bait, before sunrise,
south coast of Molokai.

Left: Planting taro, Waipio Valley,
Island of Hawaii.
Below: Harvesting taro root, Waipio Valley.

browse neurotically in straggling dry grass. People on the beach at Makena opposite Kahoolawe will every so often see a puff of red dust spring up as a beast bites into a butterfly mine and shreds himself.

Away along the chain to leeward, on uninhabited Laysan, guano diggers gutted the island. Feather hunters in a single strike early this century killed more than 300,000 birds, mostly albatrosses. Rabbits and hares, brought in by some low-level visionary who said he wanted to start a cannery, ate every blade of grass and all the small bushes and drove most of the birds out of their nesting places. The island started to blow away. Scientists there in 1923 saw the last three birds of one native species killed in a sandstorm.

When Cook came, those interesting Hawaiian honeycreepers were everywhere, from the mountain slopes down to the trees along the shore. Then in 1826 a ship in from Mexico dumped a barrel of bad water on shore at Maui. The water contained mosquitoes, the mosquitoes carried a kind of malaria that would kill the honeycreeper. These days the mosquitoes own the air up to about 2,800 feet above sea level. The honeycreepers do not come below that line.

This has been the story all along: the advance of introduced species, the retreat of the native. The Hawaiians brought one kind of rat with them. Westerners brought other kinds, then the mongoose to keep down the rat. But the mongoose, it turns out, does not care this way or that about the rat. The two pests – one on his way home, the other on his way to work – nod politely to each other, and the mongoose goes off to eat the eggs of native birds, and in sunstruck moments gnashes at golf balls forsaken in the rough.

The mynah bird, imported a century ago to control cutworm in the canefields, immediately sent raiding parties to the city. He has become a delinquent, sharp-eyed and impudent, quite without social conscience, congregating in thousands to waste time in the banyans at dusk, unsettling people for hundreds of yards around with his top-of-the-lungs brainless shouting.

A good many other bird cries are now not heard at all. In the Red Book of Rare and Endangered Fish and Wildlife of the United States, almost half the species listed are Hawaiian. Of all the birds in the world that have gone extinct in modern times, about fifteen percent are Hawaiian. The state bird, the nene, the Hawaiian goose, has been brought back from the edge of extinction by the most laborious effort over the last decade or so. But every time a mangrove swamp is filled, a Hawaiian fish pond drained and dredged for a marina, a housing subdivision, a golf course – every time a military road is cut through an upland forest and half-tracks grind a habitat to pieces, it becomes just so much harder to be a Hawaiian plant or bird or animal.

Thirty years ago when I came there was a Hawaiian on the ship. He was about fifty and the first Hawaiian most of us had seen. He was stocky, hard and light brown and had worked in the Philadelphia Navy Yard for over twenty years as a rigger.

The night before we arrived I found him alone at the rail. He talked then, telling me he had not written his family for years. He had brothers and sisters and many cousins. He was no longer sure where they lived. And there were many children he had never seen. He even wondered if he would recognize his own brothers. He had written a letter a month before and addressed it to the Postmaster in Honolulu. He hoped someone had got it but didn't know. Nor did he know what to expect of Hawaii. He was still Hawaiian, but he had been away for such a long time. Maybe it had changed. He had heard of changes, he said, many changes. He was not sure he would like them, particularly if he was alone.

I didn't understand him then as well as I do now, remembering.

The change began when a white man found a harbor on the south coast of Oahu, "a small but commodious bason with regular soundings from 7 to 3 fathoms, clear and good bottom, where a few vessels may ride with the greatest safety." In a good year for the whaling fleet, more than 150 ships crowded together there, and a man could walk a mile from deck to deck and never get his feet wet. Until the age of deep-draft steamers the harbor needed no dredging. There was no other anchorage like it in the islands, nor in the Pacific for thousands of miles in any direction.

The harbor made the nondescript native village of Honolulu a capital city in just over half-a-century, though the first haole to take a ship inside the reef there got no thanks. William Brown was a Britisher, one of those enterprising, risk-taking merchant captains who sailed in the fur trade between the northwest coast of America and the market city of Canton. He dropped down in the winter months to refit and refresh at the islands and peddle guns to the chiefs. Brown christened his harbor Fair Haven, mixed in the native politics of Oahu, and died of it on New Year's Day, 1795, when his Hawaiian allies stole his ships, murdered him, and carried off his body.

Honolulu grew up a seagoing city, smelling of bilgewater, sandalwood, sperm oil, manila cordage, oakum, molasses, and spilt rum. After dark the loudest sounds were ships' bells by the score telling the watches of the night and the oaths of liberty men pitching out of taverns on their heads in Fid Street. The first seamen's chaplain of the town used to scull about the moorings in a little boat handing up temperance tracts to larboard, for the sailors to throw promptly over the side to starboard. It was the whalerman's joy to drink his earnings, put as much extra grog as he could on the credit slate, and steal away with the tide, paying his debts at the foremast, as the saying went.

Now and then, others left who should not have. Keep your eye out, said a rueful advertisement in the Honolulu *Polynesian* in 1847, for James F. Lewis of the National Hotel, American, thirty-five years old, six feet tall, stout and well-built, swarthy, with black eyes and hair and a roman nose, wearing small gold earrings, and carrying $9,000 in specie and bills of exchange belonging to his employer. Reward $500.

People kept dropping off ships and back on, into the life of the town and out again. They stayed to be cured of scurvy at the consular hospital, or to die of consumption, enriching the doctors who padded their government accounts and kept patients on the books long after the bodies were signed out for burial in the seamen's plot at Nuuanu. There were ladies all over town pacing widow's walks on the rooftops and hanging lanterns in the windows against a husband's return. Bully Hayes the pirate left his woman, Stormbird Emma, ashore at Honolulu and never came back. She grew old and blind as a seamstress for King Kalakaua, and fell about

Late evening hillside, North Kohala District,
Island of Hawaii.

the streets soaked in gin and self-pity, hiccuping out her pious song, "Count Your Many Blessings."

Some could afford to, at that. Honolulu's oldest business house began with two young sailors, James Robinson and Robert Lawrence, who arrived in 1822 on a schooner pieced together from the wreckage of their ship, broken up on Pearl and Hermes Reef hundreds of miles to leeward of Hawaii. They took four months in the lagoon there to build the schooner and another ten weeks to make Oahu, with nothing but a battered quadrant and a pinchbeck watch to guide them and just three gallons of fresh water left when they let go anchor. They built the first wharves at Honolulu, started a shipyard at Pakaka Point, and made a fortune.

Robinson and Co. ran itself like a ship for half-a-century. The main office had a wooden figurehead, bells rang in the works every fifteen minutes, and just before noon all hands downed tools to splice the mainbrace. Bobby Lawrence, who left the Point infrequently, Oahu only once, and the islands never, always kept a bit of tarred rope in his pocket. When later on one of the Robinsons went to live at Frog Lane away from the harbor, he built a house with no electricity or other modern gadgets, no nails, everything wood-joined, to look like a ship.

The harbor made the town, and the town made the islands. Hawaii has always turned its money around at Honolulu, with sandalwood for China in the early days, whale oil and bone brought in later from the northern Pacific for transshipment to the east coast of the United States, sugar for a century after that, pineapples in quantity for the last fifty years or so, and now the newest, most lucrative harvests of all, soldiers and tourists.

One way or another, it has been enough to go ahead on.

Look up Queen Street as far as the customhouse, said the newspapers in the optimistic 1850s, and the salty part of the town is like one of the great marts of the world, teeming with merchants, ship chandlers, brokers, pilots, boardinghouse keepers, porters and reporters, car men, boat boys and natives. All the business of the waterfront goes on everywhere nonstop.

The wigwag telegraph on Diamond Head signals a ship offshore. The town loafers pile onto the lookout above the post office, straining to get a glimpse of a great clipper out beyond the reef, scudding by in a cloud of canvas, all sails set for China. A sidewheel steamer comes nervously inside through the narrow channel, pushed and shoved along by the belching harbor tug (named, inevitably, *Pele*). And aground in a tavern, a brine-pickled old whalerman delivers himself of some judgments on steamer captains: a race of silk-stockinged, pomatum-anointed, white-gloved, musk-scented gentlemen, better suited to play Miss Nancy than command a ship. What do they know? Well, for one thing, says the paper, they know how to get a cargo from Honolulu to Boston or New York in a hurry.

Go into the counting houses along Merchant Street, and see what Honolulu is really up to. You will see how dirty work makes clean money, what part whale blubber, oil, bone and ambergris play in the political economy of man and woman–"how many extremes meet in that ultimate relation which connects the ambrosial beauty of Fifth Avenue with that floating manufactory of perfumes, that singular compound of horse-pieces, bilge-water and cockroaches, the whaleship."

I am fond of curiosities often finding essence in them. One favorite, a sailor's verse, I ran across at the Lyman Museum in Hilo, in a glass case filled with odds and ends of scrimshaw – the carvings of sailors long months at sea. Likely it accompanied a piece of whalebone corseting, the gift of a New Bedford or Nantucket man to his faraway love:

> *"Accept, Dear Girl, this busk from me*
> *Carved by my Humble Hand.*
> *I took it from a Sperm Whale's jaw*
> *One thousand miles from land.*
> *In many a gale has been the Whale*
> *In which this bone did rest.*
> *His time is past, his bone at last*
> *Must now support thy breast."*

Another favorite comes from the old Pioneer Inn:

> *"Rules for This House*
> *1. You must pay you rent in advance.*
> *2. You must not let you rent go one day back.*
> *3. Woman is not allowed in you room.*
> *4. If you wet or burn you bed you going out.*
> *5. You are not allowed to gamble in you room.*
> *6. You are not allowed to give you bed to you freand.*
> *7. If you freand stays over night you must see the manager.*
> *8. You must leave you room at 8 a.m. so the women can clean you room.*
> *9. Only on Sundays you can sleep all day.*
> *10. You are not allowed down stears in the seating room or in the dinering room or in the kitchen when you are drunk.*
> *11. You are not allowed to cook in you room.*
> *12. You are not allowed to drink on the front porche.*
> *13. You must use a shirt on when you come to the seating room.*
> *14. If you cant keep this rules please dont take the room."*

The real difficulty with the blubbery trade, and sandalwood before it, was that they could not be depended upon. Sandalwood fever ran high for several years until the mid-1820s. When the demand was hottest, the commoners spent more time in the mountains with axes than they did keeping up their taro patches. The chiefs made sure of that. On credit, they were buying Western fancies – pleasure schooners, billiard tables, crystalware, big houses built in Boston and knocked down for shipment round the Horn. Then, suddenly, the huge stands of trees were all cut out. The chiefs were depleted, left with debts to be paid in wood that just was not there to be harvested any more.

In the whaling business the only certainty was that one year in five was apt to be a disaster. Once, in those same optimistic 1850s, the kingdom's treasury got down to $453.24. And in the best of times, whaling was still seasonal. Commerce at Honolulu, said the papers, was a hibernating animal that had got things mixed up, gorging itself through the fall and spring whaling seasons, dozing and licking its paws in the summer. For weeks after the first ships of the northern Pacific fleet made port and offloaded their barreled oil, arrival and departure times were of the first importance. But if in July or August the big public clock on Kawaiahao Church tower ran down, it did not matter much. Three merchants playing cards all the drowsy afternoon in a doorway could have the entire Chamber of Commerce for an audience. The biggest financial gamble of the summer might concern the chances of one trader being able to wheel another home half-a-mile in a barrow for a bet.

It took a blithe attitude toward debit and credit to

Right: Family graveyard, North Kohala, Island of Hawaii.
Far right: Kalahikiola Mission Church, North Kohala,
Island of Hawaii.

Above: Onlooker at State Legislature opening,
Honolulu, Oahu.
Right: Kawaiahao Church, downtown Honolulu, Oahu.

get through times like that. Even substantial men might crack. One pious merchant who convinced himself that he had not done conscientiously by his shareholders spent his last years barricaded in his bathhouse, praying and endlessly scrubbing his hands. Another, after thirty years of recording in his diary the business ups and downs of the port, the $500,000 spring and fall whaling seasons along Merchant Street and the $2.30 summer Thursday afternoons at his store, lapsed at last into the strange perceptive poetry of the insane: "These days run uphill – other days run back again . . . We touch the verge of the lamplighter . . . It is strong ungovernable was very ungovernable."

So it was, so it was, and never more than when the whaling industry passed away in the 1860s and 1870s, dead of the Civil War, of disasters in the Arctic ice and oil wells dug on the American mainland. But the toughminded and adaptable survived. The smart, enterprising money went into plantations. Sugar, heaps of it, hundreds and then thousands of tons, poured into the troughs and valleys of the financial year. In 1869, for the first time, Hawaii managed a favorable balance of trade, and for the better part of a century after that, it was sugar all the way.

Hawaii's natural market was the United States, of course, and the men in Hawaii who did best commercially were, as often as not, Americans. All the nations of man passed through the islands and the thing was to make common coin of heterogeneity. The quickest to learn the trick, according to a somewhat disdainful Englishman, was the "rapid, intelligent, all-sided" kind of man that "the social hotbed of the United States produces so quickly and in such numbers – a man, who

if his practice as a surgeon fell off, would become a merchant; if he failed at that, would become an editor; or, meeting with disappointment in the last vocation, would without hesitation climb the steps of the rostrum as a preacher; and even at a pinch would offer himself as a candidate for the presidentship."

Such men, believing they could do anything and be right whatever they did, were apt to take over the running of affairs. There was a gold corner in Honolulu the same year as one in New York. The organizers were among those who pushed to have the Hawaiian kingdom joined to the United States by a treaty of commercial reciprocity in the 1870s, for the sake of the sugar market. ("Except sugar and dollars," wrote Isabella Bird Bishop, "one rarely hears any subject spoken about with general interest.") In the 1890s, for the sake of good government and good business, the improvers were for annexation. To turn the islands into American soil was the greatest improvement, the greatest victory. It was won in 1898.

Where there are winners, there are losers. If the harbor made Honolulu, and Honolulu made the islands for the haole, the effect on the Hawaiians was something else again. Quite unawares, every ship that hove to off Honolulu and fired a cannon for a pilot was declaring biological war. The natives who went out laughing on the reef with hawsers, to warp merchant ships and whalers to safe mooring, hauled in death hand over hand.

Measles or influenza or scarlet fever would kill a Hawaiian just as readily as typhoid, cholera, smallpox, leprosy or plague. All these came in at the ports, and so did venereal diseases. Cook's men left syphilis on

Niihau. Coming back to Maui and Hawaii at the other end of the chain less than a year later, they found the sickness there ahead of them – it had traveled the islands at the rate of a mile a day.

When Captain Cook came, the Hawaiians numbered something like 300,000. A century later there were no more than 50,000.

Twice a year, the Hawaiians made a new makahiki on sailors' money. They came to the ports to greet the whaling fleet, and there was no keeping them away. There was dancing in the taverns of Fid Street, a great tousling of blankets in the brothels of Cow Bay near Iwilei on the bad side of Honolulu and along Rotten Row in Lahaina. And in the back streets one of the briskest businesses was the making of plain coffins.

Sitting in a friend's house one night, we were talking of the old times and places, and a Hawaiian who was there told of returning with his daughter to Maui where he was born and had lived his boyhood.

"We went up into the valley, to the old place," the old man said, "and everything had disappeared as if taken away on winds. All the houses, even the church. Only a few stone wall fragments and weed-covered grave mounds were left. It was very sad for me. I looked down the long valley to the sea and I thought of the land emptied and I wondered why we ever leave such peace and loveliness."

Nothing was more clear than that the city, the haoles' world, was bad for Hawaiians and was likely to kill them, no matter how much they enjoyed living there. Native land and native people wasted away together at Honolulu, as the separate rational private plans of white men compounded themselves into public irrationality. By the 1870s, the watershed of Nuuanu was in ecological anarchy. The hillsides were denuded, and every time it rained heavily, millions of gallons of water sluiced straight to the sea. Floods and freshets began to assault the town. Lakes formed at street corners, houses sprang leaks, adobe walls crumbled, and down Nuuanu Valley, borne on rushing waters, came big logs from timber yards, flimsy laundries and bathing houses from the banks of the stream, spars, abutments, even complete wooden bridges. Occasional drowned animals went by, feet up and bloated, and here and there the coffins of Hawaiians, washed loose by the storm.

The sad thing was that the country offered no certain refuge either, at least of the old kind, because the city was pulling the country out of shape as well. Young women went to town to dance and make love and a little money. They might come home, they might stay and keep house for a foreigner. Young men shipped out from Honolulu or Lahaina on whalers. They might wind up beached somewhere else in the Pacific. The big plantations getting started after mid-century were owned and run from the city, for profit. The soil disappeared and the ohana, the family rooted in the soil, was pulled up by the roots.

Somewhere along the line, the saddest of balances was tipped. The Hawaiians came to think of themselves as doomed. The haole could count himself lucky. The land had not been made for him, but he had succeeded in making it his. For the Hawaiian, the old song was ending. To the kings and queens who succeeded Kamehameha the Great in the nineteenth century, only the merest handful of children were born, not enough to perpetuate the dynasty. The Kalakauas who followed were barren too. More often than seemed natural, the chiefs died young. Time and again, the heavy funeral processions set out at a slow march with flaring torches and doleful chants from the churches of Honolulu to the mausoleum in Nuuanu. And the commoners – the commoners spent more on funerals than on weddings.

Gaily, eyes sparkling, old Kawena Pukui sat at the head of her valley and chanted the multiplication tables in Hawaiian, rippling, rhythmic vowel music. Her arms lifted and she made delicate, gentle hula gestures with her shoulders and hands. Then she stopped and laughed and I with her.

"When we were small, we did that to have fun. We made songs and games out of so many serious things." Her eyes *went soft, then she remembered my question, and shrugged.*

"You ask of morning," she went on, serious again. *"First there was Kumukahi, the rising place of the sun. Kakahiaka was the name for morning and Awakea was noon. Auina la,"* she said. *"That was the name for afternoon. The place where the sun set was Lehua and Ahiahi meant evening. The name of darkest night was Po. It was also the name of the world of lost and wandering souls."*

Was there a name for twilight – dusk, I asked.

"Oh yes. That was Molehu, the time of ash light." She *paused and looked down into the valley.*

"That is where we older ones are now," she almost *whispered. "Molehu." Then she began again. "After night fell,"* she said, *"there would be no work. It was time for rest and talk. Later, when coffins came into use, it was particularly bad to do any work at night that required hammering. Because the pounding sounded like coffins being made, a bad sound. There were no undertaking parlors where we lived, you see, and the coffin was made right in the yard. I remember the sounds of my grandmother's and my mother's coffins being built."*

Hawaiian society was disintegrating, and hardly anybody would have been interested to put it together again, even if they had known how. Only the Protestant missionaries had a plan: God's plan, they were certain, but very much a New England plan too. These good smalltown men and their tidy wives were more of those same rapid, intelligent, all-sided Americans – but with a conscience.

In civilized Hawaii, conscience was far to seek. The merchant mariner coming into the Pacific hung his on Cape Horn, to be reclaimed on his way home. If the Hawaiian had trouble counting and measuring and figuring percentages, and would cut more sandalwood than a contract called for, well and good, even if commoners cutting for months under the lash of a greedy chief lost their health and their ordinary taro-patch livelihood. If a Hawaiian seaman would work harder than a white man for less money, well and good again. The white man was a kolea bird. All he wanted to do was roost at the islands, fill his belly, and leave, heavy with prosperity. What did he owe the native that concerned him half so much as what he owed his creditors in the United States or Europe?

The Calvinists approached Hawaii another way. They came freighted negligibly with everything except piety. Conscience was their cargo. And learning. And industry. They were God's handymen: farmers, carpenters, printers, doctors. Lacking wealth, they overflowed with plans for making something out of nothing, and not only for themselves, but for the Hawaiians – stone meeting houses and wooden sugar mills, village industries and yeoman farms, textbooks and testaments and land reform schemes and constitutions.

They were a new sort of improver, then, improving occasions as well as freeholds, finding lessons everywhere, though they were rather better at teaching than learning. There were things about the islands that they never got over. They came from hand-hewn houses on flinty New England farms, where in winter cattle trembled in the snow and potatoes were rock-hard. They had a tendency to see Hawaii in black and white rather than body-brown or the primary colors of nature. One of the first missionaries prepared himself for the islands by religiously eating bananas on the ship. He never did get to like them, any more than native Christians could bring themselves to eat baked beans with good grace. Then there was the little missionary boy who at his first glimpse of the palm trees of Waikiki burst into terrified tears. And then, of course, there was so much blithely visible flesh to be abhorred, gay flowers in the hair to be reprehended, frivolous pastimes and impractical good humor to be schooled to sobriety, so much to do to translate Hawaii into the sound terms of New England. Civilization is inhibition.

The Protestant missionaries numbered only a dozen or so to begin with, husbands and wives, and at the height of their influence never more than a hundred, in a population of some score thousand. There was holy presumptuousness in their proposal to save Hawaii. Still, American Puritanism has always been famous for this. Calvinism is strong medicine, and those who thrive on it are likely to go about congratulating themselves on their special personal rigor, making others uncomfortable in their antiseptic presence. Whole societies have been known to prefer the sickness to the cure. Considering the particular sweet ailment of the gentle Hawaiian nature, the Protestants had great successes.

Half their ideas did not work, half did. An excellent average, in a blundering world. They were here so early, from the 1820s on, and they had so many ideas that the genuinely civilized institutional part of Hawaii – the part having to do with schools and churches and representative government – can be said to have been mainly their idea. All this is no mean monument.

Yes, the kahus still exist, my friend told me. They are guardians, keepers of the sacred places, the burial caves of the alii, the temples of old. Almost always they are old people – in areas not easily reached. They may live as farmers or fishermen but they also live a greater responsibility.

How can you tell who they are? I asked him.

Usually it is an old man sitting alone, he says. He has finished his work of homage, cleaning the sacred place, and he is sitting by himself after his labor. He may even be chanting, but silently. You will not hear it. Most times he will be neatly dressed, in respect – this old man sitting by himself in a field, a lonely place.

How does one talk to him? I wanted to know.

Quietly, pleasantly, with no show, no anxiety, he answered. And you must never fold arms or hold your hands behind your back or place them on your hips. These are signs of arrogance and disrespect, even if not meant to be. A Hawaiian will understand, but he is very sensitive to gestures. An old one speaks a great deal with his hands and his eyes. The movements of fingers will have meaning to him. It is best

Above: Spear fisherman with island lobster, Makena, Maui.
Right: Maui youths, evening gathering, Makena.

Birthday luau, Makena, Maui.

to stand with hands hung by the thighs. And you must never ask direct questions. Talk of other things, other places. One must deal in metaphors, it is the only way. When he talks you must be aware of the obliqueness of his reference. It is his nature to talk around, beneath and over a theme. This must be interpreted. Mention of trees elsewhere means trees in his land. Stones, clouds, fish, people, objects become clues to other meanings. Subtleties will emerge and understandings will be reached. You will be allowed to glance through the door of being Hawaiian – if you are deemed worthy.

Many haoles never have this experience. Their minds are too cluttered with tidiness, too well-ordered with education. They are too lacking in poetry and too obvious in such poverty, and the Hawaiian knows it and his mind is forever decisioned about you.

The Hawaiian David Malo lived in himself the history of his people, in their contact with the merchant and the missionary. Dead a hundred years and more now, Malo was a remarkable man, far and away the most piercing intelligence among the natives of his day. He was more acute, for that matter, than all but a very few haoles, and those few only because they had learned the ways of the large world earlier than he. No one ever worked harder to come to terms with what was happening between brown men and white men.

He was a favorite of the chiefs. He knew their songs, dances and amusements, and he learned their genealogies, their traditions, and the intricate workings of the kapu system. For years he had the reputation of knowing more than any one else about what Hawaii was like before Christianity.

This walking wellspring of pagan authority was con-verted in 1828. No mission ever made a more perfect Calvinist: severe of temper, harsh of judgment, strong of passion and prejudice (so ran his obituary, written by a missionary), yet, "allowing for all imperfections . . . an extraordinary example, of the wonder-working power of the Gospel, together with the accompanying appliances of education, upon natives of these Islands." Consumed by a pious lust for useful knowledge, Malo enrolled in his thirties at Lahainaluna School. He helped form the kingdom's first constitution, sat in the first national legislature, and was the first superintendent of schools. He composed dirges for dead chiefs and wrote the classic description of Hawaiian antiquities.

He grew his own cotton, spun it into thread and wove the thread into cloth, cut his own suits, and wore them with "conscious satisfaction." He made good molasses and bad marriages. He was married three times and widowed twice. His third wife was much younger than he, and did not take life seriously. Malo prayed, and she went to the bad with sailors at Lahaina. He beat her with a "small stick," and held onto the haole faith. He helped translate the Bible into Hawaiian, reproved native backsliders, was licensed to preach the Gospel, and ended his days an ordained minister of God.

Malo was a man of great accomplishment and greater promise. Inside the resourceful young Hawaiian, it would seem, was one of those rapid, intelligent, all-sided Americans just waiting for the nineteenth century to let him loose.

And yet it is not as simple as that: Hawaii is never simple. Malo might lament that when the commoner was released from servitude to the chiefs he turned into

Overleaf left: Onlookers at Duke Kahanamoku funeral, Waikiki, Oahu.
Overleaf right: The Reverend Abraham Akaka carrying ashes of Duke Kahanamoku for burial off Waikiki Beach.

113

an indolent layabout. But at the same time he hated the thought that haole industriousness would eventually make the islands haole altogether. The older he grew the more he found himself in his heart of hearts to be Hawaiian, Hawaiian.

He never did bring himself to speak English, and that alone says a lot about him. He started too old, said the obituary: "his vocal chords were too stiff and unmanageable to allow him to utter English sounds." But that was not it, really. Whatever others may have thought was the reason, he did not want to foul the pure native sources of his expressive identity. When it came to the point, he choked on the noises haoles made.

One of Malo's missionary friends used to say of him that he was "fifty years before every one in the islands." This meant that Malo could not help but be an unhappy man. He could see what was coming for his people. Dying in 1853, he asked to be buried above the tide of civilization. His grave is high on the slopes of Mount Ball beyond Lahaina. It can be reached, but you must go on foot. There is no road.

We were at camp deep in South Kona one night. Our fronts were warm from the fire. Around us it was cold and black. It was a night for stories and this is one Wayne Collins told:

"*I was hiking, high up in the ranch country. It was when I was with Fish and Game and I had some reason for being there – a bird count or something like that. It was cold and I was working along through a depression in the pasture, taking it easy, certainly thinking I was very much alone, then suddenly I heard a noise and looked up.*

"*There was this Hawaiian, on a horse, and he held a rifle on me. It was a Winchester '94, of all things, and the man was glowering. I stopped, there were more hoof scrapings, and soon there were about eight of them on horseback, all with rifles and all Hawaiian or part-Hawaiian cowboys. And they looked upset and serious.*

"*I just stood there, wondering what the hell was going to happen. One of the last to arrive was an older man whom I knew slightly. He said something in Hawaiian to the others and they rode off, waiting at some distance. He got off his horse and walked down to me. He didn't waste any time in pleasantries. In effect, he told me I was a good guy and he was a good guy and he didn't want to see me get hurt. He said all this in a roundabout Hawaiian style but there was no mistaking the message: I was going where the Hawaiians didn't want me to go and I was to leave, right then, and stay away. There was no explanation. That was it, and they watched for a long time as I went back down the slopes.*

"*I have no idea what they were guarding. It might have been an old burial place of the chiefs, or a temple site or religious shrine of some sort, I don't know.*

"*The curious thing is that I'm not sure they knew. I've often wondered about this. In the ancient system, the kahu, the guardian, had a sacred charge. And it was passed on from generation to generation. It was a great honor to be keeper of hallowed places.*

"*But over the centuries it seems almost certain that the sites themselves would be lost or buried – by earthquakes, flash floods, lava flows. A grove of trees that held great significance in long ago days is now dust. Nothing remains. These men may be simply guarding memories of vague places. But it doesn't matter. It is a great privilege that they are the Selected. And they will pass the commission on to their children and children's children and the youngsters will know even less...*"

V Plantings

Not every Hawaiian had it in him to become a David Malo. But eventually as many as one in four of the vanishing population became church members, and some of these made a separate peace with modern times.

Charles Nordhoff, walking through the Puna district of Hawaii in the 1870s, came across one such man, a farmer laboring in his sweet potato patch, a minor Malo. "He took me," Nordhoff wrote, "to the most curious and barren-looking collection of lava you can imagine, surrounded, too, by a very formidable wall made of lava, and explained to me that by digging holes in the lava where it was a little decayed, carrying a handful of earth to each of these holes, and planting there in a wet season, he got a very satisfactory crop. Not only that, but being desirous of something more than a bare living, this man had planted a little coffee in the same way, and had just sold 1600 pounds, his last crop. He owned a good wooden house; politely gave up his own mats for me to sleep on; possessed a Bible and a number of other works in Hawaiian; after supper called his family together, who squatted on the floor while he read from his Scriptures; and, after singing a hymn, knelt in family prayers; and finally spent half an hour before going to bed in looking over his newspaper. This man, thoroughly respectable, of good repute, hospitable, comfortable in every way as far as I could see, lived, and lived well, on twenty or thirty acres of lava, for which not even a Vermonter would have given ten cents for a thousand acres; and which was worthless to any one except a native Hawaiian."

Nordhoff's man had found a refuge – in a place others judged to be without value. He gave entry only to so much of the outside world as he wanted to, surveyed the rest across his lava wall, and scratched dignity from the soil. He might persist in cultivating Hawaiian tradition, but only at his loss. The outside world was writing off his culture and telling him that what he held in his heart and soul was not worth much.

Public places of refuge, established largely on the missionary plan, began to appear. The Lunalilo Home for aged Hawaiians, the bequest of a king, was set up in Honolulu proper and moved to the outskirts of town when land values rose. The Hawaiian Homesteads were established, designed to turn every willing native into a Nordhoffian farmer on lands unusable for sugar. (A place is something that can be bought up, and in Hawaii, where land is at a premium, the sale is likely to be made.) The Kamehameha Schools were endowed out of the crown lands of the dynasty, run generally by white trustees, and just now, after eighty years, are beginning to teach Hawaiians that their culture might once more be a rainbow arch to life rather than a sheltered dwelling cave. The last refuge, after all, is something unbuyable – a *sense* of place.

Often I have been confused about Hawaiians. They seem to move in and out of focus, and have different views of themselves and what has happened. It appears I am not alone.

The Hawaiian historian Kamakau:

"... in ancient times ... the bones of the unprincipled people could not be hidden ... The bones of the wicked would be exposed ... abused and dragged about on the road and become a sight to strike fear. This is not so now, for the bones of the wicked and the bones of the righteous are all together in one burial ground ... today the bones of the wicked are safe; no difference is seen.

"Perhaps the reason why this bitter fate has been taken away from the wicked is because of the introduction of law. By law, the whip is applied to the wicked and they are imprisoned while living. This may be the reason and it may not be."

Other missionaries followed the Protestants. Each, no doubt, saw part of the truth. Each claimed to have it all. Each failed in the end to show the Hawaiian a truth that would save him and still allow him a sense of himself. The Catholics were less demanding than the Protestants on matters such as smoking and drinking and eating luau dog – things which are as consequential as you make them. The Episcopalian bishops were known to watch a hula without a burning sense of sin. The Mormons at Laie on Oahu found a way to get Hawaiians to work the soil happily for profit.

The Protestants, though, were closest to the government of the kingdom, and they were the ones who were consulted when new land laws were framed in the middle of the nineteenth century. If the ohana, the extended family, had been made the landholding unit, the Hawaiians might just have saved themselves in their own way. But the provisions of the great land division, the Great Mahele, aimed at creating, in the mass, a kind of Hawaiian who never was and never would be, Nordhoff's man and David Malo notwithstanding.

The prescription was for a working yeoman, individualistic, sober even in his amusements, strenuous, yet at peace with himself in dignified labor on a kuleana, a one-family plot. In that century of imported certainties, it seemed indisputably best to the Protestant lawgivers – acting as always in what they took to be the best interests of the natives – to clear the companionably crowded hut. Get those scores of casually visiting fingers out of the poi bowl and those comfortably ensconced buttocks off the sleeping mat. Put everybody and everything in the proper place. Send people about their business. Civilization is separation. That has always hurt the haole less than the Hawaiian, for whom separation is pain.

It was left to the planters to make new sense out of the disturbed relationship between man and land, to bring a settled seasonality once again to the broken rhythms of life, to make the earth productive again. Enough white men were broken in the early years of systematic agriculture, trying to make silk, sisal, cotton, coffee, tobacco, and indigo into staples for the islands. The rest took up sugar, the one crop likely to survive the Old Testamental insect plagues that afflicted newly plowed and cleared land, and make a market overseas.

Successful planters in Hawaii were like nineteenth-century entrepreneurs on the American mainland, tough, competent, imaginative, self-confident men, all side-whiskers and expansive vests and cigar smoke in the banker's office, all booming polysyllables in their prospectuses, all work-boots and whipcord and monosyllables on the job. They were capable of seeing the most prodigious industrial and commercial leaps of faith as calculated risks, then making calculations stick.

Samuel Alexander and Henry Baldwin, two missionary boys, went into the sugar business on Maui. They had a few thousand dollars, most of it borrowed. Their plantation was flat and dry, not worth much. Baldwin was manager, sugar-boiler, engineer, and accountant, and paid himself $100 a month. "Rain, health, reciprocity and God's blessing," wrote his

Above: Cane fields from air, Kahului, Maui.

Below right: Sugar cane in morning, Ka'u District, Island of Hawaii.

Below left: Canefield worker, near Lahaina, Maui.
Below right: Loading treated cane for planting,
Honokaa, Island of Hawaii.
Right: Loading harvested cane, near Lahaina, Maui.

father hopefully, "will get you out of debt." The reciprocity treaty went through, the market went up. Then Baldwin caught his right arm in the rollers at the mill and had to have it taken off.

There was plenty of rain in the mountains to the northeast, and the partners wanted the water for their cane. To get it cost them $80,000, advanced by the merchant house of Castle & Cooke, also a missionary partnership. Baldwin built the Hamakua Ditch, the first thing of its size in the islands – seventeen miles of channel, flume, and pipe, cut and laid through thick forest, up and down hills and across ravines. It was heavy going, all done by hand, and at Maliko Gulch, 200 feet straight down, the workers refused to go over the edge on lines to the bottom. So Baldwin with his one arm went first, and they followed, and got the ditch finished.

Baldwin lived into the twentieth century. He stood for hard work and the Republican Party, was for compulsory education in the islands, and played the organ onehanded in church. He was a builder.

He's in the real estate business in Honolulu now, but Bill Brooks grew up at Lahaina on Maui, where his father ran the American Factors company store. During the years he has told me much of the life and the men of the plantations.

"*Back about forty years ago,*" *Bill recalls,* "*the Alexander Young Hotel was where the plantation managers stayed when they came to Honolulu for meetings with the Big Five bosses. A few times I saw them in the lobby there when I was a youngster, and it was quite a sight, I tell you.*

"*They'd wear the gabardine-like pants with high, beautifully polished boots, white jackets – and big, broad-brimmed hats with fresh flower leis for bands. Back on their own plantations they were absolute rulers. Cane was king and they were the princes. Their word was law and no questions asked.*

"*Old David Fleming was the big boss at Honolua. He had helped convert the land from cattle ranching to sugar cane years before, and he was a rough, tough old Scot. Every night at nine he'd throw the master switch, dousing all the lights in the laborers' camp. The buggahs oughtta be in bed, was his philosophy. He was a great botanist; knew a tremendous amount about plants – and fish too, and the birds and even Hawaiian legends of the Lahaina area. He used to take me riding around with him because he knew I was interested in such things.*

"*I remember how the lunas, the foremen, would ride up to meet him on horseback and sit there, actually trembling, while he gave instructions.*

"*Years later, when I was a man, I went back and I could see him, through a window in the office, arguing about something with his son, Bruce. After a while he came out, still sore as hell. I said, Good morning, Mr. Fleming! – very pleasant. And he looked at me and grunted hello. But he was still angry; you could see he still felt the need to chew someone out. So he glared at me for a few moments. Then he barked, 'Listen here, Bill Brooks. Don't stand in one place on that grass. You'll kill that damn grass if you stand in one place. Move around, god dammit!'*

"*Then he stomped away. He wanted to say a nice hello to me but he had to show who was boss first.*"

The industry grew on steam and sweat and credit and faith and applied science. The planters and their professional thinkers broke the life cycle of the cane into stages, its cultivation, harvesting, and processing into specialist functions. A good chemist or entomologist came to be worth his weight in almost anything, and it was hard to put a price on an inventive engineer. New varieties of cane were bred endlessly and surrounded by biological controls, in which Hawaii came to lead the world. Conveyors, rollers, and centrifuges were invented, tested, developed, adjusted incessantly. Steam plows and narrow-gauge locomotives yammered and snorted their way, cheerful and purposeful, across the contoured landscape. The mills were full of racketing, whirling, flailing, chopping, grinding, stuffing, stoking, squeezing, munching, crunching black cast-iron machinery that smelled definitively of molasses and made the overwhelming, unarguable noise of economic sense.

The planters proceeded along the lines of a forceful straight-ahead, simplifying, common-sense reasoning: get as much land as possible under one paying crop – two, when pineapples came in about the turn of the twentieth century – and service the crops by requiring from as many men as possible just one thing – work. This meant, for a start, that once the plantation was invented, imported labor was inevitable.

Hawaiians were not counted out as laborers – in the 1870s one of every two native men worked in sugar – but they were few anyway by then. And they did not much like economic rationalization, private or public, small-scale or large-scale. In the days of the labor tax, they would build a bridge for the government supervisor of public works exactly as if they were treading a taro patch, with forty laughing, shouting men carrying a log that could have been lifted by four or five. There would be a woman for every man to help the hilarity along, and music for emphasis. Hawaiians evaded the other taxes of civilization, too, moving out in droves ahead of the census taker, burying their taxable dogs temporarily, eating their horses rather than pay.

Even the sophisticated natives of the city really did not feel like keeping time with business. After all the cats and dogs and chickens and church bells of Honolulu were stilled, and good haoles were asleep against an early start at the store, here would come a native brass band, twenty strong, trumpets and trombones and an indefatigable bass drum, playing beneath the windows with tremendous expression, "Put Me In My Little Bed." No dying people ever stepped to such lively funeral music. Plantation workers, though, had to be up at four-thirty, in quantity.

So labor would have to come from somewhere else. But where? There were many kinds of work no machine could do, most of them sweaty and tedious. And matching men to work loads was a most approximate science. It was understood that the Anglo-Saxon would never perspire for plantation wages, bent over in the hot sun with hoe or cane knife. If you wanted Europeans, they would have to be (so the prescription of the Minister of Immigration went) "just low enough to make them contented with the lot of an isolated settler and its attendant privations." In practice this meant Portuguese, mostly from Madeira and the Azores. Otherwise it meant Orientals, peasants: two kinds of Chinese, the Punti and the Hakka; Japanese from Yamaguchi, Fukuoka, Kumamoto, and Hiroshima prefectures; some Okinawans from the Ryukyus;

124

Below left: Experimental pineapple seedling,
Pineapple Research Institute, near Wahiawa, Oahu.
Below right and bottom: Newly planted pineapple,
Dole Plantation, Lanai.
Right: Young pineapple in field near Wailuku, Oahu.

a handful of Koreans; and four kinds of Filipinos – Tagalog, Ilocano, Visayan, Pangasinan.

"We kids all played together," Bill Brooks says. "Race made no difference. But there was a separation and we knew it. And at night we went our separate ways home. Being a haole was special – no doubt of it. If a haole came to the islands, he got a boss-job. It made no difference if he was incompetent or a bum or drunk.

"We worked in the cane as kids, yes, but it was like being the boss's son anywhere: you did your time in the lower echelons for training and experience. There was never any doubt that you'd move up, get out of the fields.

"My father took me once to Salt Lake City when I was about fourteen, and I remember seeing a white man digging a ditch near that seagull monument they have there. I wondered what a grownup white man was doing, working with a shovel like that. I asked my father about it.

"He told me that on the mainland it was different. That white men had to do that kind of work there because there were so many of them. Not like in the islands."

Over the years between mid-nineteenth and mid-twentieth centuries, something like 400,000 workers were recruited. Something like 300,000 stayed – about as many migrants as there had been Hawaiians when Cook came. The planters went looking for a labor force; they created a new population.

No one intended this, exactly. Most Orientals probably had some version of that universal, sad, optimistic migrant's dream of going home after the undefined fortune was made. They did not mean to stay – or at least they did not give staying much serious thought, as year after year they stayed. And even if they did think about it, the planters on their side had no thought that there would ever be a place for the Oriental away from the plantations, where there would always be another crop to harvest . . .

In this view of things, there would always be a Filipino camp, with fighting cocks in cages and ripa women coming by to run their sociable lotteries for the bachelors from the barrios. The Chinese would forever grow their queues, play fan-tan demoniacally after work, or drift off serenely and illegally in an opium cloud, coming down next morning good-tempered, shrewd, vocal, wordly, rational, practical, level-headed as usual. The Japanese, on and on, would go naked and companionable to their communal bath, lie about bonelessly in intimate gossipy clusters in the scalding water, then present themselves for work again, clothed, stiff, inaccessible, unconformable figures, wiry-framed, baroque-legged, those steady eyes unreadable in faces looking like masks of themselves.

This was what most white men saw. If there was more to the Oriental than met the eye, they did not search it out. The planters were all amateur sociologists, but only industrial sociologists: one kind of migrant was good for this sort of work, another for that. Here and there a plantation haole might wonder if one of those strange inarticulate men brought his real self to the slogging, repetitive work of the fields or left it at home in the camp hut by the Buddhist shrine. Or, for that matter, if he had left most of himself at home.

What did the Oriental want? What sense was he making of Hawaii? This might offer food for thought. But by and large the planter was not that kind of thinker. He was not paid for it. The puzzle hardly even had to be reduced to its component parts, much less solved, as long as there were crops to get off, as long as the workers filed in and out of the camps ranged below the great house, from whose grounds each morning the manager issued on horseback to set the labors of the day in motion.

"An old man who came to work as a junior plantation boss back in the old days was telling me how it was in the 1920s," Bill said. *"Early, before dawn, it was colder than a witch's tit on that high Hamakua Coast. He said he'd hear his neighbor's alarm clock go off, followed by a goddamit; then the grunts and sighs as the guy roused himself. The walls were only boards. You could hear everything.*

"In a few minutes there'd be the pop of a cork and he'd hear the other fellow gurgling some whisky. Then a nice long Aaaaaaah, when the booze hit. Next came the patter of bare feet across the floor, the noise of the water tap running, and shocked grunts and groans from the cold of it.

"After that came the loudest, the worst noises of all – when a man had to put on clothes still icy-wet from the day before. This was almost always followed by another cork-popping and gurgle-sounds and soon they would all gather for breakfast. After eating, they'd mount up and be off in their own directions for the day – miles away.

"He said they looked like ghosts, riding off in mists of early, early morning. And most of them had jugs stashed away in rock piles or tree roots along the way, for warmth."

"Not until much later," wrote Armine Von Tempski, a girl who grew up in a big house on the hill, "when I visited the sterner lands of more northern latitudes did I realize what a wonderful heritage was ours – the children of white parents born and reared in Hawaii . . . my comrades were polyglot . . . Ah Sin, the Chinese cook, whose mummy-like face, whose oaths resounding like gongs, invested him with the qualities of a magician. Tatsu, my Japanese nurse, who always warmed her hands inside her kimono before touching me, and who smelt faintly and pleasantly of incense and pale hot tea. Makalii, the old Hawaiian paniolo – cowboy – who carried me on a pillow in front of him while he made his daily round of the near pastures, who taught me the lore of his people, who schooled me to understand the whispered language of nature."

Oriental cooks and nurses were all very well in their place. A plantation would not have been a plantation without them. But there was a special relationship between this kind of country-born haole and the Hawaiian, and most of all the Hawaiian on horseback. Those scores of thousands of cattle running wild on Maui and Hawaii were an invitation to ranching. (One of the most surprising things about these small islands is that a quarter of the land is under cattle, and Parker Ranch at Waimea on Hawaii is as big as any privately owned spread in the world.) In the 1830s some Mexican vaqueros – Spaniards, paniolos to the Hawaiians – came to teach herding and cutting and lassoing. The natives took to horseback work with delight. They got themselves good Mexican saddles, red bandannas, and sombreros. Those who were really serious about being Hawaiian cowboys wore flower leis on their hats (pansies, of all things, planted by one of the two tough haoles who started Parker Ranch). They gave their saddles a hand-stamped mark of their own design, just as

Above and right: First-generation
Japanese-Americans, Honolulu, Oahu.

Far right: Plantation worker's house,
Waialua, Oahu.

the old people used to mark their tapa cloth with family patterns. And they had a pair of spurs handmade by Constant Fortrain of Honolulu, who could get the finest musical jingle from beaten iron.

The best local paniolos turned out to be as good as any in the world. Ikua Purdy, descended from the pansy-planter and his Hawaiian wife, went by invitation to Cheyenne, Wyoming, in 1908 for the world steer-roping championship ("Bring your own saddle and lariat; horses provided"), and won.

There was more than something in the idea that the happiest Hawaiian was the native paniolo. After he got his Fortrain spurs, what more did he want from the city? The horse lifted him off the ground, put him close to nature, gave him a way to turn his subtle perceptions and fleeting impulses and superb reflexes into sweeping motion. He had found out how to surf the land. That was happiness. For Armine Von Tempski, the night always came alive at Haleakala Ranch on Maui when the paniolos, decked with flowers, rode up in the dark on their best horses to serenade the big house, with a shouted song of allegiance to the beautiful open island and the rolling uplands of the soaring mountain that came "bursting from strong brown throats and big brown guitars." And from the heart. Kilakila o Haleakala.

"To people who have never been with Hawaiians," she wrote later on, "it may seem absurd to say that their very presence is healing. But Island-born whites know what I mean." This was the same little girl who used to wish that she were half-a-dozen people instead of just one, so that she would never miss a thing going on at Portuguese Camp or Japanese Camp, or any-

where at Haleakala. The Hawaiians, though, healed her, made her whole.

"There was an old Hawaiian in Lahaina when I was a boy," Bill Brooks tells. *"His name was Kekoa. It was accepted that he was a kahuna. He lived in a grass house and had his own shrine with its kuula, fish god. Kekoa liked me and gave me a Hawaiian name, Mana, meaning spirit. I was too young to know it was an honor.*

"He told me several times of a stone fish-god that his grandfather had seen. The old man had told Kekoa stories about it when he was a boy, but Kekoa knew only it was somewhere, hidden away, on that coast, probably along the cliffline at Pohakuloa – Windmill Beach. Kekoa said that in the olden days, fishermen from Lanai and Molokai had come all the way to Maui to make offerings at the shrine for it was a very sacred place.

"I know that such stories are enlarged and changed as they pass from generation to generation, but this one stayed with me. For seventeen years I looked for that kuula, even after I moved to Honolulu. When I went home, I used the free time to explore the cliff. Over the years, I climbed it again and again – and it stretches about a quarter-mile, rises up from a thin, stony beach to about 150 feet in height.

"One afternoon, I was inching along a narrow ledge around forty feet up, and I noticed at my feet some coral scraps and black smoothworn beach stones. I know I passed them many times before without thinking, but that day I asked myself, 'What are they doing at this height? It must have been a helluva wave to toss them this high.' And I bent down and saw they covered a recess. Carefully, I cleaned away the scraps and I got a chill up my spine as the god-figure slowly came into view. A heavy stone, with

eyes, nose and mouth. I was so excited I was trembling.

"Man, I tell you it was a job – moving it out. It must have weighed fifty pounds and I moved real slow, foot by foot up to safety, hugging it. I took it because Kekoa told me when I was a boy, 'If you are One with the spirit it will find you.'

"So I had no fear of moving it, and it is in my house now."

The island haole, without necessarily knowing that he is doing it, has always turned for a sense of self-completion to the Hawaiian. Everything the white man is not, the native must be. (So this reading goes, and it does not matter that it may not be demonstrable: that it has emotional truth is what matters.) The Hawaiian is the man the haole has left behind along the urgent, changeful, littered highway of progress and accomplishment. The white man, pausing to take stock of where and who he is, finds himself clever in complexity: the native, by contrast, seems wise in simplicity. The white man has a cold, rational passion for finding things out; the native has a warmer certainty about values. The white man is master of civilization, the native is at once child and king of nature.

So for the haole, the Hawaiian – even the deracinated one of the nineteenth and twentieth centuries – has his subtle and essential uses. The native, in every white man's secondhand dream of surcease, has come to embody a version of humanity less complicated and constrained than the one brought into being by Calvinism and capitalism.

The Hawaiian, for his part, came to believe at least one thing of the haole – that he would provide. Or at any rate that he ought to. If the kings were gone, if the feather cloak was hopelessly tattered, why should not the Hawaiian lay a claim on the good feelings of the new alii, the white chief who had title to the lands?

When Bill Brooks was a boy they had an old Hawaiian working for them who had been a coachman for King Kalakaua. That had been the only big thing in his life.

"He wasn't much use," Bill recalls. "He was so old that he actually didn't know night from day. In the middle of the night we would hear whistling and singing outside and there he'd be – out raking leaves or working in the yard.

"He was the only awa drinker I ever knew. If he couldn't get the awa he drank pineapple swipes. The awa made his skin scaly, I remember. When he got drunk, he'd slip away for days. Someone would find him under a tree and say, 'That's Father Brooks' man.' And they'd bring him back to us. My father never said anything to him . . ."

Early this century, after American republican revolution and Hawaiian royalist counter-revolution, after white victory and native acquiescence in defeat, at a time when even the city answered to the sugar and pineapple plantations, there emerged a special kind of haole-Hawaiian solidarity. It is waning now, with the plantation era – another island song that is ended but remains good for a chorus or two. Most haoles here these days arrived too late to have any idea of what the song has been about. They have no land, any more than the Hawaiian; they themselves must lease a house lot from one of the big estates. And most blood-Hawaiians do not allow their consciousness of their genes to shape their attitudes too rigorously. They would be foolish if they did. Like everyone else who lives here, they are blessed with an extraordinary spectrum of choice in

Preceding spread: Cattle roundup, Greenwell Ranch,
Kona Coast, Island of Hawaii.

Below and right: Bull and horse sale near Waimea,
Island of Hawaii.

Above left: Hawaiian paniolo, rodeo parade,
Makawao, Maui.
Above right: Onlooker, Makawao rodeo parade.
Right: Paniolo, Makawao.
Far right: Calf-roping contestant, Makawao.

styles of life. Once, though, that solidarity was powerful and binding. On the strength of it, and under the right circumstances, a haole of good family might marry a Hawaiian of good (and preferably land-owning) family, and suffer no social odium. Brown-skinned men of the proper sort might even join certain very selective haole clubs.

I like the story all the more because, undoubtedly, someone made it up . . .

In the 1930s, two businessmen were standing and chatting on a streetcorner. A hapahaole, part-white, waif approached them shyly and the men looked at him smiling and indulgent. "Can I have a dime, Daddy?" said the lad, eyes downcast.

And both men reached in their pockets . . .

What was being proposed, in essence, was that the Hawaiian should have a haole patron, a sponsor. And not just at the club. Under the territorial government, Hawaiians by the hundreds – by the thousands, even – became politically minded functionaries: policemen, firemen, janitors, civil servants, clerks of court, bailiffs, wardens, graded, ranked, uniformed, entrusted with a certain authority, grateful to be able to invoke modest power with a jingle of keys or the thump of a rubber stamp, delighted as well to be seen tempering authority with geniality.

For years, one of the street sights of Honolulu was a personage known as the Hula Cop, doing his officious, finger-wagging, traffic-directing dance at a busy intersection. If you do not want a ticket, keep your eyes on the hands.

And on the vote. Another version of the haole-Hawaiian union created the Republican Party, an alliance based upon two ways of looking at the same things. A belief in land as the source of life, or at least in fee simple as the source of influence. An acceptance of hierarchy as a natural organizing principle of society. A strong feeling that mutual dependence would mean comfortable co-operation. All this went into the local version of political conservatism, and race added its special coloring.

Politics became a taro patch to tread, a log to roll. There was luau pig in the pork barrel. The campaign rally went local, with singers and dancers for garnish. Hawaiian political hyperbole had a special charm. No serious candidate would be without his name chant. Television has all but done this in, as it has so many things. Still, who would not have voted for Mr. Samuel E. Kalama, Republican, twenty years county chairman of Maui:

"The mountain-dwelling birds are startled
By the great eagle soaring aloft.
Joyous news has been heard,
That Kalama reached the highest point
And made the banners of victory float on high
Over all the districts of Maui.
His enemies were as naught –
Those with evil and unkind hearts,
That sound like fiddles
Without charm to attract sweethearts,
The enemies turn to each other
To ask what caused their failure.
Perhaps the kahuna went off his course
In his observations of omens in the sky.
They were held down by the mana of his ancestors

And the Trinity from above.
The cloak of the runner waves in the aeloa breeze.
The victorious candidate of the Republicans,
Kalama stands forth in triumph,
Adorned in roselani leis,
Denoting Maui's excellence.
This ends our praise,
A song to adorn you, O Kalama.
Again, another ending we sing,
Hipa hipa hipa huro!
Hip hip hip hurrah!"

Haole-Hawaiianism reached its apotheosis on the island of Niihau off Kauai. The Sinclair-Robinson family bought the place from the kingdom in 1864 for $10,000 and ran it for most of the next century as a private preserve. Their Hawaiians worked cattle, took their education in their own language, sang pre-Darwinian Protestant hymns, did not travel much, were happy in their refuge, failed the armed services literacy tests, and cast their political votes faithfully. The ballots were flown by carrier pigeon to Kauai for counting, whereupon it turned out that the Niihauans, Hawaiian to a man, were also, election after election, Republican, Republican, Republican.

"U.S. Grant McCoy, let's call him," a Honolulu oldtimer said in telling me the story. "He still has lots of grandkids and great-grandkids around. God knows how many. He came to the islands in the late 1800s on a sailing ship, started to deal in land, and built himself a fortune. And he was one of those guys who had what the Hawaiians call manao – the spirit and feel of the Hawaiian. Not too many have this gift – that's what it is – and Hawaiians know it

immediately and respond to it. So, along with money, McCoy had himself a lively life.

"He began to take a lot of 'wives'. It was a funny thing because he was not really good looking. They say his angle – if you can call it that – was to sit silent and look sad. Hawaiians can't stand a man looking sad, so first thing you know the women would be taking care of him and trying to make him feel better, then wham! – he'd be 'prouncing' them, as the Hawaiians used to say. No one ever did figure out how many wives McCoy had, but the story goes that at one time he had six illegitimate boys on the police force alone.

"He served in the legislature at a time when the haole plantation owners dominated a House that was almost a hundred percent Hawaiians. Running for office once, he accused his opponent of being a mule. 'He cannot reproduce himself,' McCoy said. 'He has no children. Is this the kind of man the Hawaiians want to represent them?'

"The other man admitted what McCoy said was true. He was not a father. But, he said, the Hawaiians were not electing a man to place him at stud. 'Keep McCoy home at stud,' he suggested. McCoy's answer was that he could easily handle all the political problems in a few months every year and spend the rest of the time with his friends and neighbors. The implication was clear and he was overwhelmingly elected.

"When McCoy died, his legal wife refused to let anyone outside the immediate family attend the funeral. All the other wives raised hell, pleading for a look at the body, so she allowed it to be placed on view at a mortuary downtown. They say it was quite a scene. The Hawaiian Princess at that time wanted to know what was going on and sent a spy to the funeral parlor. The woman came back and said there was a terrible wailing and thirty-seven wives had been counted crying over McCoy's corpse. A wag at the Palace is

Right: Hawaiian women, Honaunau, Island of Hawaii.
Overleaf: Iolani Palace and member of Kaahumanu
Society, in old Palace mirrors, Honolulu, Oahu.

supposed to have said that the number was small because a lot of McCoy's wives couldn't get in from the outer islands."

In the Hawaiian-haole interracial embrace there was hardly any emotional room for the Oriental. He had no invitation to join. He did not yet seem suitable. On the plantation he was everywhere part of the landscape. Yet he still wore a specific, detached, remote, unassimilable look. The faded photographs of the time show Japanese women field workers masked against dust, gloved against blisters, bundled into alien shapelessness. The men hold themselves with a tenseness far beyond any cameraman's instructions not to move. The pictures say what everyone was taking for granted. These people are outsiders. The men cannot be pictured on horseback like plantation haoles. They are not apt for whipcord and leather and instinctive command of broad acres. Neither do they stand with the easy planted familiarity of the barefoot native. The land is not theirs by birth. They do not have their homes and lives and beginnings and endings here. They are not born. They materialize at the immigration station, go through quarantine and disinfection, are assigned to Camp 4, and perform a function.

They were curious, unique people, the oldtimers . . . In Kohala on the Big Island there's an old New England-style house. It's in ruins now, a few old sticks of smashed furniture and the windows all broken out. The family probably left in the 1920s sometime. But there is still some sort of fund in existence to maintain the grounds and the lawn. The house is falling down but the surroundings are neat and nice. It's up around Hawi, in the old Union Mill area.

Bill Brooks and I went into it once and there were some paper scraps on the floor. I picked them up and you could still read the lists: "Strikebreakers: 4 Hawaiians, 2 Koreans, 3 Japanese, 6 Chinese," and so forth. No names, just so many bodies and their races.

That's the way it was then, Bill said.

In town, where plantation earnings gave prosperous men a taste for spaciousness, the Oriental had his place as well in the planned landscape, the calculated decor. Most of the city rich of Honolulu went in for some sort of Gothic revival house, often considerably gingerbreaded, or for rambling, ramified, three-generation homes of clapboard, with wooden pillars and wide verandahs called lanais, owing about one-third to New England, one-third to the plantation South, the rest to the Hawaiian climate.

The banker Samuel Mills Damon went further. He was a connoisseur of cultures with an eye for display. The Damons had missionary connections in the islands and in China, and Samuel's brother Frank started an excellent school for Orientals in Honolulu. (One of his students was Sun Yat-sen.) Samuel's estate at Moanalua, just to the west of the city, was an entire ahupuaa, running from mountain to sea, willed to him by the heir of the Kamehamehas.

Damon turned Moanalua into a great park, "with most perfect trees, beautifully kept lawns, cascades of flowering vines from immense heights grown in wooden frames by an imported Scotch gardener." There were some Hawaiian fish ponds, a thatch house, a natural salt lake, and a golf course on which Damon never played. He collected Hawaiian artifacts, "antiquities" already by the turn of the twentieth century. He imported a Japanese carpenter to put up a house – "the Japanese Samurai House in miniature – though large enough to live in," with "many toy-like rooms with their beautiful shining floors, their embroidered screens, bamboo shutters and paper walls." It was in perfect taste, visitors agreed. Outside were bonsai trees, giant Japanese ferns with leaves like spread hands and a place where you could refresh yourself with "water from a dear little fountain, drinking from a bamboo cup."

Or you could take tea with Damon and his wife on a weekend afternoon in another house, made in Canton for shipment to Honolulu. It was a work of art, sitting on the edge of a tiny lake, "its pagoda roof sloping gracefully over its sides and its doors standing hospitably open. The hand-carved frieze around the ceiling, the inlaid ivory, the onyx tables, the Chinese teakwood furniture and handiwork of all kinds, with the tiny elaborately gowned Chinese maids flitting about serving tea at long koa-wood tables – really . . . " said the lady visitor, almost running out of words.

The Dillinghams were another family of business princes, doing things in a big way, not averse to creating effects. The first of them, Benjamin Franklin Dillingham, left his ship at Honolulu in the 1860s with a broken leg. He stayed to make his million opening up leeward Oahu to plantations with artesian water and railroads and planned immigration. Later, the family company got the big contract for dredging Pearl Harbor, and turned the vast, impenetrable coral maze into safe anchorage for the United States Pacific Fleet.

La Pietra, the fine home of Walter F. Dillingham and his wife Louise, at the foot of Diamond Head, was a walled Italianate villa, Medicean in scale and inspiration. Walter and Louise lived well and with flourish, entertained a lot, and were famous for it. La Pietra was filled with Renaissance urns and Tang horses and Persian wine jugs and Flemish tapestries. "I have a theory," Mrs. Dillingham used to say, "that the best and finest from one country harmonize with the best from any other country. And, do you know, I think the same is true of peoples, too." The names of princes and poets and senators and generals were in the guest book. There was power in the air and fine talk at table. The food was served by silent Japanese maids in kimonos. The lawns were clipped by Filipinos. All was right with the world.

"My oh my," the elderly lady on Maui says, remembering for me from her worn velour sofa surrounded by the bric-a-brac of a century. "It seems so long, long ago. Oh yes yes," she says, "it was lovely, bright and colorful when the men played polo. Almost everyone on the island came and lined the field – and the horses and grass, everything was beautiful and gay. There were the Baldwins of course, all very good players, and David Fleming and E. C. Lindsey and the Rices. Each island had a team and they came over frequently to play, and after the games there were parties. The Army had a team and they came. General George Patton played, and I can tell you, the air was blue when he didn't like something. Oahu had Walter Dillingham and Harold Castle among others, and once Will Rogers played here too.

"We had many parties and picnics, and the Fourth of July was always a big celebration on the minister's front lawn. There were dances and people played a lot of dominoes and there was the Ladies Guild to aid the churches. When we had the dances, there was a piano and sometimes a violin . . ."

Below: Miss Mabel Wilcox, at home,
Grove Farm, Kauai.
Right: Manager's home, sugar plantation,
Olaa, Island of Hawaii.

VI Harvests

"What is the business of Honolulu?" asked a planner brought in from the mainland at the turn of the century to advise the locals on beautification. "Yours is not, and does not aspire to be, an industrial or a great commercial or financial city; it is that rare thing, a city of delight, seeking to give leisure and pleasure; flaunting, not volumes of black smoke, but green hills and blue seas, the rainbow and the palm. And if your business is to give pleasure and be beautiful, you can afford in unwonted measure to be conservative about changes, to shun the 'checker-board' plan as you would the plague, and to retain the narrow, winding streets . . . Cut through broad avenues and boulevards, build a hot and sunny quay, widen your streets and straighten them . . . and when all the work is done, the winsomeness of Honolulu will have departed, and it will always be spoken of as the town that was spoiled."

When this man wrote, canefields came all the way in from the central uplands of Oahu to Moanalua; there were vegetable gardens all through Kapahulu and Manoa; Kaimuki was mostly red dirt, Waikiki mostly duckponds. Still, the business of Honolulu was – of course – business. In a short time all those places would be built up. And downtown, one man's winsomeness was always some other man's chaos.

Honolulu grew by annular rings outward from the harbor, and the center of the downtown district was left a dreadful firetrap. Along those narrow winding streets the water supply was uncertain; fire engines had no room to maneuver. There were years when no sensible insurance company would issue a fire policy.

The rutted, potholed thoroughfares were arenas for tests of nerve between riders and drivers of differing persuasions. Foreigners bent on business saw virtue in holding to the side of the street they used in their home countries. Natives out for pleasure rode not to or from, but about–anywhere. People kept a running tally of the kings, chiefs, diplomats, and ministers of God hurled from their carriages on impact with the ox-carts of barrel manufacturers and hardware wholesalers. The private interest kept crashing into the public interest.

Still, business got done. Banks and churches rose, the plantation companies reared financial fortresses, built imposingly and to last. By annexation, times were good.

That year, 1898, the first automobile, a Wood Electric, arrived to frighten the horses; it was followed by the first gas-engined car in July, 1904, the first steam car a month later. Hawaii had its first fatal automobile accident in 1906. Who would have thought that in the 1960s winsome Honolulu would have as many cars per head of population as any town in the United States?

Lewis Mumford, planning for the city in the 1930s, granted the problem of traffic but allowed Honolulu a fair chance of survival still. With a population of 150,000 the place was overgrown, he thought, but not horribly so. Bishop Street, with the harbor framed in palm trees at the lower end and a view back to the mountains, he thought potentially one of the fine business streets of the world.

He hoped the city would do honor to the sea with a few more avenues such as a beachfront boulevard, and keep the cool trade winds blowing across the business district unimpeded by high buildings. Let the city breathe and stretch itself in green open space, and all would be well, said Mumford.

Out among the canefields, the haoles had their own

plan for the countryside as well. Simply put, it was that the year 1900 should go on forever. Time, of course, was against any such thing: time, the ending of labor contracts, and a new sort of migration within the islands. Countryside and city could not be kept apart.

No plantation worker coming to the end of his term had made his fortune, or was likely to. Not many, at a few dollars a month, managed to save a fare home. And neither the government nor the planters wanted the expense of paying the worker's way out of the islands. So, beginning with the first Chinese coolies, a good many laborers left the plantations, and made a China-town at Honolulu. This led to the bringing in of Japan-ese, hired to stay more reliably in the fields. They too left for town. So did the Filipinos in turn. The planta-tions kept growing, but only because more and more workers were shipped in all the time. And almost as soon as Chinatown was named, it was misnamed, as anyone could see. Except for the haole, almost every kind of person was living there.

This most intractable by-product of agriculture, this mountain of men – no one had a plan for its disposal. The industrial planning of the planters was as efficient as could be. How the whole of society was to arrange itself was more problematical: it had been the world's problem ever since the races first noticed their separate-ness, and Hawaii was having to approach it point blank.

I fell in love with her quite easily.

She was tall for a Japanese and moved with a wet litheness on the beach. There are many things I can still remember about her – her fine skin, her smile, a delicate clean soap-scent she carried like an aura. Her voice was soft and shy and gentle.

My days led only to our hours together. After work in the evenings and on weekends I went to visit, eagerly. We would walk through the darkening neighborhood, talking, talking, or sit on a grassy hillside under great trees, watching the night come. We discovered how best to kiss each other and I ached for her. But she never gave herself. Strangely now, I am happy about that. It makes the memory sweeter, that hunger.

I wanted to be married and she said she wanted it too. But she came from an old-style Japanese family. Her parents would be terribly upset to know she was even seeing a haole. You must wait, she told me. Wait and understand, she asked.

I waited and wanted, plunging from joy to despair. I don't remember how or when it began to end. But a year after we met I was married to a haole girl. And a few months later she married a haole man.

That was nearly thirty years ago. Our children are now as old as we were when we met. The last time I saw her, across a street downtown, she looked fine, in a matronly sort of way. And I wondered what our lives might have been.

Lewis Mumford was able to make a nice abstraction of Hawaii in the 1930s. He construed out of the life of the islands a trace of simple beneficence left by the natives, a ceremonious cult of beauty brought in by the Orientals, and among the haoles a systematic rationalism, a close accountancy of time, money, energy. It seemed a promising formula for man, if only the proportions could be got right.

Mumford went on to describe Hawaii as a miniature experimental station in the hybridization of cultures. The remark about experiments was just an extension into human society of what industry was doing so

150

Waikiki and Honolulu at night from
Diamond Head Crater, Oahu.

Below: Sailors on leave, Hotel Street, downtown Honolulu.
Right: Morning traffic, Lunalilo Freeway, Honolulu.
Far right: Mosaic decorated hotel, Waikiki, Oahu.

Below left and right: Ala Moana sidewalk sale, Honolulu.
Bottom left: Shriners, Aloha Week parade, Honolulu.
Bottom right: Hawaii Raceway Park, Oahu.
Right: Newly constructed middle income housing, Oahu.

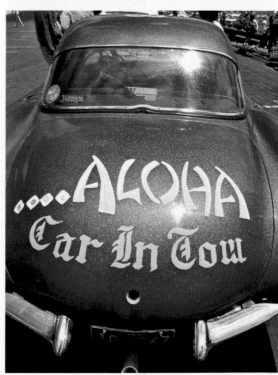

successfully with cane and pineapple. It is the kind of thing that has been said in the islands a thousand times since. It is well-meant, usually, and probably does no harm among such people as Americans, who are generally comforted with the notion that society can be engineered – scienced – into reassuring shapes. In Hawaii the difficulty is that no one ever really says who is in charge of the experiment.

"This Auntie Lou was some gal," a local businessman was telling me. *"Almost pure Hawaiian, and going into her late fifties; a damn goodlooking woman – plump, tall, with a gusty-lusty approach to life. A lot of the older Hawaiian gals are like that.*

"Once, she bought a refrigerator from me and didn't pay for it. I knew she had plenty of money and was just fluffing it off. So I called her up and she said in that sweet Hawaiian-auntie-style, 'Yes, deah. You send one man, I pay him.'

"Without thinking about it, I sent a big young haole guy who worked for me. He was about six-and-a-half feet tall, husky, a real handsome bastard.

"Three days later he came back, walking slow and with a big smile on his face. He looked tired, even thinner. I asked if he got the money and, incidentally, where the hell had he been?

"He said he had been at the 'Hawaiian lady's' house, like I asked. No, he didn't get the money, he said.

" 'But by God I got everything else,' he told me. 'Soon as I rest up, I'll go out and try again.' "

Underneath everything, beneath polite and cultured notice at least, there was in fact some hybridization going on, though no one involved in it would ever have heard the word. Cook's shore party on Niihau started a part-Hawaiian population. The whalers carried it on, without even marriage in mind. Hawaiian women, educated in time to the theory that a man should be a good provider, would consider for a husband a haole, a Chinese, even a Japanese, if one could be pried loose from his conviction that dokyo-jin, compatriots, were the only suitable mates.

These people, in the aggregate, were making a distinctively local population. With far too many single men among the migrant workers and far too many Hawaiian women cut loose from the ohana, couple after couple came to private understandings about what was worthwhile in tradition and what might be sensible under new circumstances. They were by no means social engineers, least of all in their private lives. They made the most momentous decisions about life in the inarticulate, unsystematic way of ordinary people everywhere. Important men, public men, spokesmen might feel called upon to say a few words about the way things were going or should go. The locals went their own way, in their own language.

In days when Hawaiian was still spoken widely, politicians had to employ interpreters in rural campaigning. The office-seeker would make his speech with pauses for translation.

I have always liked the story told of a Portuguese running for office on the Big Island. There was strong belief that he had fathered one of the pretty half-white girls of a certain village and his opponent "talked-stink" about the adulterous liaison.

The Portuguese man kept denying it, perhaps a little too vehemently. At the end of one of his speeches, his Hawaiian interpreter summed up faithfully but couldn't resist making an editorial comment:

". . . And he says he is not the father of the woman Kinau's child. But you and me, we have seen the girl and we know he is a liar."

The Portuguese lost the election, never really knowing why.

The point of a local language was good and less good. For each new kind of migrant, the plantations sprouted a new variant of pidgin – more unsystematic hybridization. Everybody was able to understand everybody else, after a fashion. Enough, at least, to get the work done, and that was the major part of the definition: the word "pidgin" itself is a Chinese attempt at the English word "business." It has been marvelous and distinctive in Hawaii that ordinary men from everywhere have learned to talk with each other in a homemade way. And sad that pidgin, which allowed this in the first place, went on to stop them from saying more.

Pidgin remained on the plantation with those who stayed there (and is still there), went to town with others, was passed to their children, and has become the great mark of the local boy, whatever his genes. It does not as a matter of course turn into English over the years. Involved in pidgin, rather, is a resistance movement against English. This is important. Language holds personal identity. What a man is willing to relinquish of himself, and what he most deeply wants to hold on to, will sooner or later become clear just in the noises he makes as he opens and shuts his mouth. It is a fact that a good part of Hawaiian society, since the migrants started to come, has been made up of David Malos of different races, choking on the noises haoles make.

Almost from the outset, pidgin developed uses beyond those of getting the haole's work done. But this did not necessarily bring migrant and haole together. The consummate pidgin speaker, in fact, is likely to be taking a continual subtle revenge upon haole condescension. There are piercingly witty men and genial philosophers among the pidgin speakers, and many a haole loose among them never learns, even with experience, whether he is being skewered and spitted for roasting, or, alternatively, graciously pardoned for existing.

The question then becomes who is most hurt by this revenge. The haole may be all unconscious that he is being got at. And the English speaker is bound to win, in any case, because English rules, not only in the islands but in the world to which Hawaii is now joined, politically, linguistically, electronically.

If the haole controls the territory of the word, he controls a great deal indeed. Pidgin does not lead to reading and writing – leads away from them, out of school, so to speak, thus out of power, out of society generally. In order to come to terms with the times, it is necessary to come to terms with English. To be a skilful manipulator of language has proved rewarding, as these things go. There are any number of professional local boys in business, politics, entertainment, and tourism, who play both sides of the street of language beautifully. But to be a genuine unreconstructed local boy is getting harder and harder. Such a man is more closed in even than David Malo. He feels the chafing of the chains. To be a pidgin speaker only is to be stricken with a wound that smarts all the more because it just might turn out to be self-inflicted.

The white man has always been a great measurer. He likes to set boundaries, to know where he is, and he often defines his position by announcing where others are, or where he would like them to be. In Hawaii the haole has been likely, at one and the same time, to misunderstand the alien for being alien, and to misunderstand him when he tries not to be alien. Where that has left the alien is, again, problematical. If he were to turn outward, he might become a local boy; if he turned inward, he would surely stay an alien. Hybridization was hardly the word for this. All through the first decades of this century a close association of haole business houses known as the Big Five – familially close in their organization, growing out of the missionary days – ran the larger economy as they chose, and politics as well. The other communities were defining themselves separately, and they were not fertilizing each other, just being lonely together.

On the island of Molokai there is a beautiful valley where an old Chinese lived for many years. He had the valley all to himself, cut bamboo and raised his own food and fished, living pretty well. Every now and then he would come out for a while and get drunk on wine in the village over the mountain and once when this was going on, someone asked him what he did for women in the valley all alone like that. He said everything was 'numbah one O.K.' because there was a mermaid there who came and slept with him. Especially she would come during the winter months when the rains are cold. But he said she came whenever he went to bed wanting her . . .

   On another part of that island two Portuguese-Hawaiian brothers had an argument with a Chinese about some land. They said they were going to talk it out nicely. So they took the Chinese fishing far out in the channel. And only the two boys came back. That was the end of the land argument.

   There was some talk, but this Chinese was also alone so no one pressed the case – maybe because those two were pretty rough boys and nobody wanted to fool with them.

As late as the 1930s, there were any number of ways for the Hawaiian experiment to run itself into trouble. It was all very well for intellectuals with Lewis Mumford's flair to talk about blending essences of culture. And, at that, people could at least be seen stirring, changing places. But they seemed at the same time to be standing still. They moved out of Chinatown, to huddle instead in Portuguese Punchbowl or Chinese Hollywood. Moiliili filled up with Japanese. The island of Niihau, and Hana on Maui, Milolii on Hawaii, Papakolea on Oahu, and a dozen other places were for Hawaiians.

   Each group had to work things out for itself. The Chinese Chamber of Commerce on North King Street has a mural, done by a haole, showing their kind of migrant tending the cane, coming to town in gown and pigtail, then shedding these stigmata with all deliberate speed for business suit and professional air. The strong – and perhaps unduly modern – suggestion is that Chinatown has been somewhere to get out of.

   At that, it used to be a grubby, grimy, gamy place. The poor men who cobbled up board huts and ramshackle stores had no better idea to begin with than to copy what they had lived in as laborers. The district looked like the worst of the plantation camps lumped together, built up to two or three stories and gone furiously to seed in green-painted, termite-ridden wood. Along the lines of public health, the best thing that happened to it was that it burned down in 1886. The worst was that it was rebuilt exactly the same way, to be burned down again more extensively during the plague at the turn of the century. It was built up again, and survived to take Lewis Mumford aback in the thirties. Hotel Street became the stamping ground of the armed services on liberty during World War Two. (It still has massage parlors and tattoo parlors and shooting galleries, and a Club Hubba-Hubba still functions.) Just lately, Chinatown has begun to succumb to urban renewal, which for Chinatowns anywhere is terminal. Part of the new plan is to start something called a cultural center, with exhibits from the time when the original people of Chinatown did not know they had anything called a culture, but just lived and did the best they could with what they had.

Nearing sixty, he looks much younger. He is now either chairman or a director of several large corporations, including a bank, real estate firm, a steel mill and an airline. And he also serves on many boards of community service. I asked him once how it was when he was a child.

When he was six or seven, he said, he was a typical "Honolulu Chinese poor boy." He wore short pants and was barefoot and would arise well before dawn daily to sell newspapers. Then he would walk several miles to a bakery on the waterfront and buy bread for the family breakfast. Often that was all they had; sometimes there was fruit, cheese or milk and sometimes a loaf of tofu, soy bean curd, bought with pennies earned shining shoes.

He had five brothers and sisters and his mother to help support. His father was a cook on steamships and was seldom home. The family lived in a one-bedroom apartment in the poorer section of town. When an aunt died, three young cousins came to live with them and they had to move to slightly larger quarters across the street.

"We children never knew a bed," he said. "At night, sawhorses were set up and we slept on planks laid across them – or on the floor." Through elementary, then high school he continued working. His life was monotonous simplicity: work, school, work, then school again. In high school he sold magazines, 'Liberty' and 'The Saturday Evening Post'.

But he did not come of illiterate Chinese stock, he mentioned quietly; his uncle had been a philosopher.

The respectable world used to define Chinatown by its delinquencies. Too much gambling. The police raided games all the time, and though the connecting houses of Maunakea Street never grew as labyrinthine as the tong houses of San Francisco, the speed of the gamblers' disappearance was always a Chinese puzzle. Too much opium smoking. When opium was illegal, smuggling was a scandal. When it was licensed, the scandal was in graft. The Chamber of Commerce keeps on show now an ornate old opium bed, hard wood, with marbled panels evoking clouds for the drifting mind to play among. And too many unseemly funeral processions. To the offended ear of outsiders, the Chinese were excessively noisy, even in death, gonging and cater-wauling and fire-crackering their way across town to their cemetery in Manoa.

As an extension of all this, the Chinese, first on the ground in Chinatown, were farthest along with the sort of arrangement designed to give the migrant the sense of having left home as little as possible. Family man, villager, clansman, Punti, Hakka – years after the migrant came to the islands he still understood himself best in those terms. If a man's family still lived in Ngai How village in the Chung Shan district of China, he

Above: Island Chinese playing role of his father
for motion picture "The Hawaiians".
Right: Motion picture set on Kauai, Honolulu Chinatown
in 1800s, filming "The Hawaiians".

Left: Editor, Chinese language newspaper,
Honolulu, Oahu.

Below: Wo Fat Chinese restaurant,
downtown Honolulu.

Below middle: Cooking char siu, Maunakea Street, Honolulu.

Below right: Chinese buddha, Kwan Yin Temple,
near Foster Botanic Garden, Oahu.

Bottom: Chinese medicinal herbs in pharmacy.

Bottom right: Young's Chinese noodle factory, Honolulu.

could go to the Wing Sing Ho store on Hotel Street and have someone write him a letter home, with a few dollars enclosed out of filial obligation. He would not write the letter himself because he did not know how. He would not use a bank to send the money because that would mean filling in forms. He would not send the letter through the post because the mails in China were bad or nonexistent. The store, for a price, would see that the letter got there, and that the answer was kept in a wire rack behind the counter until claimed.

The pigtails and bound feet are long gone from Aala Park, and the park itself has already been urban-renewed. But the district as a whole is not yet caught in concrete and culture-amber. Until it is, the backroom bakers will go on pressing their designs by hand around the edge of almond cookies. The tentacular mops of cuttlefish will hang drying in the open market. The herbalist will consult his calligraphy-covered wall of wooden drawers and reach down ginseng and dried beetles and tiger balm and powdered deer horn. And everything will be for virility, health, long life, prosperity and happiness.

The Chinese of Chinatown were numerous enough to cause concern and hostility from time to time, but never sustained fright. That was the specialty of the Japanese, who became the authentically felt Yellow Peril of the islands.

It was a matter first of numbers, then of values. The Gannen-Mono, First-Year-People, 148 of them, came to Hawaii in 1868. After that, no more until 1885. The Japanese Imperial government was making up its mind how much it wanted to do with the outside world, and on what terms. These things more or less established,

30,000 workers were shipped to Hawaii in the next ten years. Then, when it became clear that the islands would soon fall under the labor laws of the United States, another 64,000 by 1900. Then, in a hurry, because the American government was showing signs of wanting to limit or even cut off Japanese migration, another 77,000 by 1910. Given the heavy demands of the sugar and pineapple industries, all this made economic sense (just as it made sense to turn to Filipinos after Japanese ceased to be available, and to bring in 125,000 of *them* by World War Two). But when all the figures were counted up, between 160,000 and 180,000 Japanese had come to stay. Many arrived with their families, and 10,000 bachelors got themselves picture brides from the homeland. By the early 1920s, a third of the population was Japanese, as was every second baby being born in the islands. All this on American soil.

The Japanese were defined by their delinquencies as the Chinese had been before them. Respectable people were always "seeing in the papers" that the Japanese were misbehaving, even though the sociologists' figures showed that no one people broke the law less often. The casual visitor to the islands, without the time or inclination to count Japanese heads, was apt to find their part of Chinatown merely quaint, and safe.

A lady from the mainland and her party could take a box at the Asahi Japanese Theater on Maunakea Street, and look up at the ceiling hung with "brocaded obis, gay sunshades, beaded slippers, bunches of paper flowers, gaudy fans, and many other pretty extravagances," and down at the locals squatting barefoot on tatami mats with their sandals lined up in front of them. The quaintness depended heavily – as it usually does – on incomprehension. There was an interpreter to help explain the whirling and posturing of the actors, but it was no use. "He told us that the play would last for hours, but at the third act we were ready to leave the plotters to their fate, since we . . . could not have told the hero from the villain." That was a problem the Japanese in Hawaii had to face for quite a while.

The question then was whether the islands had room for a Japanese community bigger by some scores of thousands than the haole community. In the 1930s this went beyond local concern. The same question was being asked about the whole Pacific. An unnerving thing was happening to Americans. Their undefined western frontier in the open ocean was beginning to look like the eastern frontier of an expanding Japanese Empire. Evidently there was no way for the Pacific to be both American and Japanese. It would have to be one or the other. And Hawaii was in the middle of the Pacific.

The local Japanese were pressed to declare themselves. Some haoles (and among them some with loud convinced voices) put them down in advance as villains. It was easy enough to do. The Japanese Empire had Westernized itself enthusiastically, and that ought to have been good, giving Japanese common ground with Americans. But the Empire was only selectively Westernized, and thoroughly militaristic. And that was bad, especially since some of Hawaii's Japanese (and among *them* some with loud convinced voices) seemed partial to marching with the Rising Sun.

It was hard to regard this as just another cultural manifestation. There were Japanese warships at Honolulu in the 1890s, looking after laborers' interests. Victory parades through Chinatown after the Russo-Japanese War, demonstrating "first-rate-power-consciousness." More of the same when Japan occupied Korea. Language papers in Honolulu and the other towns of the islands, reprinting the Imperial government's self-congratulatory official stories about Japanese colonization of the Micronesian islands and Japanese advances on the Asian mainland in the twenties and thirties. Language schools, with Buddhist and Shinto priests teaching loyalty to the Emperor, drumming the Imperial Rescript into the heads of Japanese children born in Hawaii, on American soil. These things looked like political delinquencies. The dossiers grew fatter and fatter.

If one Japanese was the same as the next – and those were the days when it was mandatory to remark that they all looked alike – Hawaii was in trouble. The census, the population projections, a head count on any street corner made that obvious. What exactly was inside each one of those Japanese heads was harder to discover, but much more to the point.

The political loyalty of immigrant Japanese might be hard to command. Certainly it would be difficult to insist upon, if for no other reason than that United States federal law denied them citizenship. Whatever they might think of life in Hawaii, a territory of the United States, they would be aliens there, by statute, until they died. The situation of their children was more ambiguous and more urgent. Japanese by upbringing, American by birth, they outnumbered aliens two-to-one at the end of the 1930s, and scores of thousands of them would be of military age when the war broke out. Some sort of declaration was needed from them. But what could they offer in evidence except their record of divided lives?

Above: Traditional Japanese musicians, Honolulu, Oahu.

Left: Japanese columbarium, fruit offering,
Kyoto Gardens, Nuuanu Valley, Oahu.

Right: Replica of the Kinkaku-ji Temple
Kyoto's Golden Pavilion, Nuuanu, Oahu.

Performance of traditional Japanese dance,
Honolulu, Oahu.

Above: Japanese Sumo wrestlers in tournament,
Honolulu, Oahu.
Right: Sumo teacher, Honolulu.

Chuck Braden was an ensign in Naval Intelligence during the early days of the war. We were idly surfcasting off Makaha a while back and he was recalling those days.

He said he was once sent to a sporting goods store in downtown Honolulu to question a young Hawaii-born Japanese employee. The lad had been to Tokyo for education.

"I got the boy," Chuck said, "and we took him to the FBI office. On the way down, we talked baseball. It was funny. He didn't seem terribly disturbed about what was happening – being interrogated and all.

"Then, during the questioning, he was asked: 'Didn't your father tell you to buy Tokyo Electric bonds in Japan?'

"He said yes, that was true. But his father also said he was going to buy an equal amount of Hawaiian Electric."

One young man, Inouye by name, was born at Honolulu in 1924, the year the Imperial government loosened its formal hold on Japanese born overseas. From then on, the children of emigrants would no longer have Japanese citizenship unless their parents took the trouble to register them at a Japanese consulate. Inouye was five times the eldest son of eldest sons. His grandfather migrated from Fukuoka province and worked as a contract laborer at McBryde Plantation on Kauai. His father went to Honolulu as a young man, scrimped his way through a Congregationalist high school, graduated at twenty-five, and got a job as a Big Five clerk.

His mother, also Japanese, was an orphan, brought up in the house of a haole, a Methodist minister. Their wedding ceremony was Christian. Inouye was born in a tiny two-family house on Queen Emma Street (opposite the Pacific Club, which did not admit Orientals and would not for another forty years or more). He was given two names: Daniel, for the Biblical prophet much admired by his mother, and Ken, a Japanese word meaning builder, so that he would build the family.

As a little boy he was impressed with his grandfather's splendid Japanese shaved head and wanted his own hair cut off. His grandfather and father did the job ceremoniously; his mother was absolutely appalled. The hair grew back; his grandfather gave him a consolation gift, a samurai sword. When he started going to English-language kindergarten his parents stopped speaking Japanese at home, but for eleven years he was sent after regular school hours to a language school for instruction in Japanese tradition. At McKinley High School (full of Japanese and called Tokyo High by haoles), Inouye the poor boy was enraged at the way the well-shod, white-shirted, get-ahead Orientals aped haoles. In his eleventh year of language school, 1939, his eleventh year of listening to alien talk of the divine wind of Japanese destiny blowing over Asia and the futility of American interference, he got enraged when the old teacher-priest ridiculed the Bible, stood up to argue, and was thrown out bodily. He never went back.

Inouye's war began the same way as everyone else's, with dreadful black clouds boiling over Pearl Harbor in the Sunday morning sunshine of December 7, 1941. For five days he bandaged wounds and stacked bodies at a school turned into a morgue – mostly Japanese from his neighborhood, killed by American anti-aircraft shells that failed to go off in the air and fell on Honolulu, exploding on impact.

Hawaii went under martial law. Fifteen hundred Japanese, mostly aliens, were interned: less than one percent of the Japanese population of the islands. The language press went silent, the language schools were disbanded. Kimonos and geta disappeared. It took a year for the federal government to decide that Americans of Japanese ancestry, AJAs, should be allowed to go on active service. Volunteers were called for in January, 1943. It was time to make a declaration.

The AJAs fought together as the 100th Battalion, then as the 442nd Regimental Combat Team, commanded at first by haoles. Inouye went with them. He learned the laws of probability in crap games, and the random conclusions of war in combat in Europe. He was wounded, then commissioned on the battlefield, and then, less than three weeks before V–E Day, he took a German rifle grenade front-on at a range of about ten yards. It tore his right arm away.

The casualty rate of the 442nd was three times that of the average American unit. As a group, the AJAs were the most highly decorated soldiers in the Army. Their regimental motto was pidgin: "Go For Broke." The unit's official history carried the title *Americans*. The declaration had been made.

Bill Brooks and Carlos Rivas have told me about revisiting Lahaina just after the war. Both of them were still in the Navy, it was their first time back in years and there was a lot of aloha. Too much, Carlos recalls. "One stop after another, seeing friends, a drink or two at every stop.

"That night, someone insisted on taking us to a luau in Puukolii – a little plantation settlement up past Lahaina. The party was in honor of about sixteen or eighteen Nisei soldiers who had just come home. It was special, because every boy who had left the town had survived – not a single casualty – and that was unusual. Most places in Hawaii,

no matter how small, had lost at least a few men.

"The celebration was held in the rickety old community center and the place was packed. Everybody in town showed up. The veterans sat at a table over the basketball center-ring. They were crisp in their uniforms, pants tops tucked into high combat boots, and they seemed pleased but embarrassed by the whole thing.

"The plantation manager dropped in with a few subordinates and he made a proper speech. He welcomed the boys home, said they were glad to have them back. He used all the cliches you could think of – patriotism, defense-of-democracy, Old Glory, you-have-proved-you-are-good-Americans, and so forth.

"Then it was time for one of the Japanese boys to answer. There was a problem getting a spokesman. Finally they pushed one fellow to his feet.

"He fumbled around, scratching his head, rubbing his face, looking at the floor. Finally he got started and everyone listened respectfully. He said thanks, and told of the places they had been, mumbling awkwardly in pidgin-style. There was Wisconsin for training – that was lousy-place. Then Sicily – no good either. Rome was good and Paris too – plenty fun. After that, London and New York, then California and home.

"Then there was a pause as he looked around at the plantation bosses and the townspeople. There was only one way to say the rest and he said it:

" 'You know, we been plenty place . . . see the worl' . . . We left Puukolii long time . . . An' I gotta tell you folks . . . Puukolii get nothin' for us now!'

"He sat down and he and his buddies were all looking at their plates. It was almost painful. I don't think anyone applauded and it took a few minutes for the party to get

Below: Father and son on Prince Kuhio Day, Molokai.
Right: Little leaguers, Waialae–Kahala, Oahu.

Below: Schoolchildren dressed for Makahiki Festival,
Waimanalo, Oahu.
Right: Schoolteacher, Makahiki Festival, Waimanalo.

Left: Graduating class, University of Hawaii, Oahu.

Below: Grandparent at Graduation Day,
University of Hawaii.

going again. By the time it did the plantation manager had gotten up and walked out.

"Most of those guys knew us from years back and one turned and hollered – 'Hey – haoles! . . . Come . . . Come drink with us!' So Bill and I went over and sat down with them. They had a case of whiskey stashed under the table. Then it began. The bottle went round and round and we were singing a pidgin chug-a-lug song. After the first few bottles were gone, I suddenly realized that it was a contest. Those Japanese boys wanted to put us haole Navy guys under the table! It was in good humor, but a real bout, serious. We drank and sang, drank and sang some more. People went home and hours later several guys were passed out on the table or under it; the table was a mess, empty bottles were busted on the floor. Somehow, Bill and I held our own. It was if they were dedicated to some kind of crazy, beat-the-haole ritual, showing us that things had changed. It was strange because we had all known each other as kids.

"It went on for hours. Around three in the morning I was really stoned. It was all I could do to keep my head up.

"One of the last things I remember is looking around that hall. It was in gloom and quiet, except for us . . . seemed empty . . . Then, through a booze haze I could see the figures, in twos, threes, fours spotted all around the hall – little islands of people. They were the mothers, fathers, sisters, brothers, wives of the Japanese boys. They had been sitting there, like dark statues, motionless and silent, simply staring, waiting patiently all those long hours for it to be over – so they could take their boys home."

On his way back to the islands, after eighteen months in military hospitals, Dan Inouye stopped in a town outside San Francisco for a haircut. He was wearing the uniform of a captain in the United States Army, with four rows of ribbons including three Purple Hearts and the Distinguished Service Cross, and there was a hook where his right arm used to be. The barber stopped him at the door. "You're a Jap and we don't cut Jap hair." One way and another, it has been hard for people like Inouye to get an American haircut.

That was California, of course, where all Japanese were interned at the start of the war – men, women, children – where a whole minority was deprived of livelihood, property, dignity, the chance to affirm itself; where it has taken a generation for public opinion and the courts to concede that wrong was done.

The same quarter-century in the islands has been a marvelous one for the sons of migrants. Hawaii is now a state of the union, and Dan Inouye is a member of the United States Senate.

This has been social revolution. The war – or rather the peace – got it started. Quite apart from the education that battle offered, an Oriental veteran could get a college education under the GI Bill, and a law degree might start him off in local politics. That was the way Dan Inouye climbed, and dozens like him.

Not many of these men were likely to be Republicans. The war, in short, brought together the makings of a Democratic Party in Hawaii, one which could contest elections and win. In the post-war years, the Democrats went out of their way to be open racially. It was this more than anything else that undermined and went some distance toward breaking up the power of the old haole-Hawaiian Republican alliance. The votes were in those same population figures that used to cause such concern before the war. By 1954 the

Democrats were in power and have remained there.

This had to happen. The alien's son had become a citizen, first by birth and then by battle. He was present in great numbers. Any number of things in turn combined to interest him in exercising his citizen's rights. And when he did, he could not be denied. The political world was his. The Democratic Party was an institution whose time had come.

The same was true of the labor movement. It gained strength first among longshoremen in the 1930s, was bitten off short by martial law after Pearl Harbor, came alive again as soon as the war ended, on the waterfront and then on the plantations.

Again, the point was that the union organizers saw strength in multiracialism. The leader of the International Longshoremen's and Warehousemen's Union, Jack Hall, was haole, his membership mostly Hawaiian, Chinese, Japanese, and Filipino. Management had always seen strength in centralization. Hall managed to match it. There were some strenuous collisions, but by 1949 labor was strong enough to win strikes and influence political elections. Since then, Hall has seen his laborers become as well paid as any in the world. And, remarkably, the ILWU here, which began and grew in high militancy, has made something of a working peace with management, so that industry on the docks and the plantations has been able to modernize and mechanize itself, stay competitive, and keep Hawaii prosperous.

Union leaders and management men, Democrats and Republicans, spent the 1950s educating each other in the new politics, the new art of the possible. And in the years since then again, the 1960s, the newest possibility of all has disclosed itself. People, ordinary people, began making the same sort of decision about politics as they and their friends had been known to make about marriage. The fact of race is undeniable, its importance considerable, and yet it is possible here to take it into account without being ruled by it.

Nearing forty, she has her beauty, with a face that combines the best features of her Japanese-Hawaiian ancestry. She owns a bronze warmth, a softness over strength.

She was born in a plantation village, in a shack with a dirt floor. There is a bank on the site now, and she herself holds a master's degree in education, is married to an American-Japanese and has three children.

When her father, a pure Hawaiian, married her mother, a finch-like, shy, eighteen-year-old Japanese, there was much talk. People said no good would come of such a union. It was doomed. Their children would wind up in the gutter.

That was a long time ago. And as doubts melted away, the family grew in love and sun and the children did well, despite the dire prophecy. Of six families on her father's side, his was the only one with children who all became college graduates.

So much for the gutter, smiles Kuulei.

The results of all this have been interesting. The new establishment is numerous, open, pragmatic, opportunistic. It has not run Hawaii on the rocks. It has not brought in a golden era of statesmanship. We have become that rare thing, a multiracial democracy which works. Being a democracy, we get the politicians we deserve. They happen to be of all colors.

Another exciting possibility appeared after the war:

Below: Voter at Republican rally near Naalehu.

Right: Republican council candidate
Wing Kong "Winkie" Chong, Honuapo Bay,
near Naalehu, Island of Hawaii.

Far right: Republican campaign truck presenting
between-speaker entertainment, Honuapo.

Left: Governor John A. Burns before annual Molokai
Canoe Race, Hale-o-lono Harbor, Molokai.
Below: Canoe paddlers, Molokai Race, Hale-o-lono Harbor.

Left: State Legislature opening, House of Representatives,
State Capitol Building, Honolulu, Oahu.
Below: Representative Minoru Inaba.
Below middle: Chief Clerk of the House, Shigeto Kanemoto.
Below right: Daughter of State Representative.
Bottom left: House Majority Floor Leader Stuart Ho
and son, Mr. Ho's mother behind.
Bottom right: Honolulu Mayor Frank Fasi and Mrs. Fasi.

that Hawaii, a lowly Territory since 1900, might become a State of the Union. Nothing as momentous as adding a star to the flag is managed easily, and it took until 1959. Again, it was the war that established the rights of all people in Hawaii to first-class citizenship. They had been bombed, they had lived under martial law, they had sent their sons to be killed. As against this, there were some obstacles that were nuisances rather than matters of substance, but which took time to shift. The psychic distance between the islands and the mainland had somehow to be bridged politically. People on the mainland had to be assured that the islanders were no more or less likely to be subversive of American political institutions than anyone else born under the American flag. All this was finally achieved, and when Hawaii began to send its elected representatives to Congress they were haole and Chinese and Japanese. No one has been able to show that this might be bad. Hawaiians have the feeling that it is good for the United States.

A few people in the islands have not been altogether pleased by this quarter-century of miracles. Niihau voted against statehood, as everyone knew it would. People were sympathetic, but in the end they could not bring themselves to care very much. And the year 1900, being a long time gone now, there are waistcoat pockets of old haole society – refuges – where grandfather clocks tick away the intolerable seconds and every hour strikes a lament for the days that used to be, when things could be depended upon and people knew their place. These big houses are few, shrines of a vanished order, and the people who live there are guardians of – what?

But it is true in a general way that all sorts of people have trouble recognizing their children.

Willie B. is a bulldozer operator, a giant Hawaiian in the primitive style. He weighs some 365 pounds, overflowing the seat of his vehicle. Willie drives a big Caterpillar, the biggest made, but even its size does not dwarf him.

Willie handles the enormous bulldozer as a child would move a beloved toy. The Cat and Willie are one, seemingly sensitive to each other. Willie's ham hands have a delicate touch and the great machine responds willingly. It is a strange mating, the dark, ponderous Hawaiian and the immense, powerful, clanking orange machinery.

Willie's work is mostly clearing old buildings and walls for new structures to come. In effect, Willie's job is destruction. But where less sensitive men would take delight in smashing buildings and destroying landscapes, Willie does his job with compassion, even fastidiousness.

His bosses like to watch Willie: the way he nudges a wall to rubble without scratching nearby structures; the way he moves the big Cat without effort and with no wasted motion. Back and forth he rumbles, pushing, urging, scooping, and there is never an unnecessary move. The engineers have told me that few men are able to operate gigantic machinery in such a way. There is something poetic about it, one said gruffly. "Willie is a goddam hula dance in steel."

Willie has been asked about this; the construction men were curious to know if Willie knew how good he was. Had he studied or practiced his work?

Willie's answer was simple: "I just like drive da buggah."

The modern skyline of Hawaii really appeared only with statehood, which released upon the islands a flood of mainland equity capital of enormous force and apparently ceaseless flow. But there was also the jet, and it was crucial.

The first aviator ever to reach the islands from the American west coast was Commander John Rodgers in a United States Navy flying boat. He did it the hard way – one day in the air, nine on the water. Twenty-five-and-a-half hours out from San Francisco and about 300 miles short of Maui, he ran out of fuel and put down. The crew cut sails from the fabric of the wings, and set off on the last leg of the journey at about two knots, with no radio contact. They ran out of food on the third day, water on the sixth, and would have run out of islands altogether if they had not managed to rig a keel so that the plane could go off the wind a little. They wound up being towed into harbor on Kauai by a Navy submarine, 1,870 miles by air and 450 by sea from their takeoff point.

This was two years before Lindbergh. It is now some five hours from the west coast to Honolulu International Airport, where the main terminal is named for John Rodgers, and where a plane takes off or lands every minute or so, day and night.

Since Lewis Mumford wrote, World War Two and the Cold War between them have made Hawaii a military base of great size. Statehood, jets, and the warm-weather lust of mainland Americans conditionally released from their sentence of hard labor, have crowded Honolulu with four times as many people, visitors and residents. Eighty-five percent of the state's population now lives on Oahu. In the unruly overgrowth of concrete and steel and glass at Honolulu, the outlines of Punchbowl have disappeared. Houses and high-rises

nibble at the flanks of Diamond Head, and every so often threaten full-scale attack on its slopes.

Honolulu works harder than anyone would have thought possible a hundred years ago. There is a non-institution (one of many in the city) called Aloha Friday. Those who wear coats and ties all week are allowed to come to the office in aloha shirts. Women may wear muumuus. (The missionaries made this voluminous dress for modesty, but the modern point is to let the body go its own unconfined way unobserved.) Some people like the idea of a complete Aloha Summer. After all, the mean temperature varies but few degrees from January to August. Others say no to this dangerous extremism: who would ever believe a bank president with his shirt habitually outside his trousers? One firm proposes to allow aloha shirts, but tucked in. The authentic Hawaiian invitation to enjoyment says, "Letta go your blouse." Honolulu does not know any more whether it can afford that, does not know the right proportion between commerce and delight – not even now, when a lot of the city's money comes from marketing delight.

This uncertainty afflicts the tourist. No one (says a thoughtful man who came here a long time ago because he wanted to and stayed because he liked it) would think of getting at the truth about the islands through statistics. In such a place, he says, we want to see smiles, to feel the kind of joy that comes from being able to live as if one had intended all along to be born.

The visitor industry does some figuring, just the same, and very strange and illuminating it all is. Hawaii has 3.94 favorable associations per visitor, and .69 unfavorable, according to one count; or, in another

Below: Construction worker, Honolulu.
Right: Steam pile-driver, Honolulu.

Left: Castle & Cooke Building,
Financial Plaza of the Pacific, Honolulu.

Right: Structural engineer Al Yee, at far left,
and associates, new highrise building, Honolulu.

version, 5.40 favorable and .74 unfavorable, for a ratio of 7.30. This means, presumably, that tourists like the place. A great number simply find it "enjoyable," without being able to say why. When they complain, which is rarely, it is about either bad weather or "too much commercialism." Note this: Paris may be too *expensive*, Hawaii is felt to be too *commercial*. The tourist wants to sit in the sun and not be sold anything. And who could argue against that? The visitor has at least bought the idea that he will be allowed to sit in the sun. Between 1886 and 1941, the annual number of visitors to the islands went up fifteen times. And between 1948 and 1968 it went up another thirty-six times, to well over a million in a year. In 1946 the tourist spent $6.3 million here; now he spends something approaching half-a-billion dollars a year, for the privilege of sitting in the sun.

The government built the kingdom's first elegant watering place for visitors, the Hawaiian Hotel, on Alakea Street in Honolulu in the 1870s. There were irregularities in the financing, the place cost far more money than it was supposed to, and its vast expanse – forty rooms – seemed an incitement to bankruptcy. Look on the bright side, said the king's ministers then: it is a big construction project, it gives employment to many people. Yes, observed the opposition, but so did the Tower of Babel; doubtless many people were employed there, and money circulated freely, but the outcome of *that* enterprise was most unsatisfactory.

Sure enough, the Hawaiian Hotel lost money in its early years, and things were quiet too for a long time at its Waikiki annex. Waikiki is virtually all hotels and apartments now. They compete for space.

They go almost all the way down to high tide, and there is a serious question of public rights of way from the street to the sand and along the water's edge. Inland, the high-rises go back to the Ala Wai Canal. The man who bought into the first one built back from the beach in 1958, so as to be sure of an unbroken view, now has a view of four apartment houses taller than his own. This is not about to stop. In the past fifteen years, more money has been spent on construction than in all of the twentieth century up to that point. In 1969 Waikiki had 19,000 hotel rooms. In 1971 there will be 31,000, more than any city in the country has, except New York.

One Honolulu contractor who has made an enormous amount of money in the construction boom is half-Hawaiian and half-Chinese. We were talking, not long ago, about planning and progress, and esthetics, and it was obvious he does not dwell much on these things. His dedication is to the bid, the job, the payroll, the profit. He lives in a fine house. He enjoys all the rich things. Yet at heart, he is like one of his own bulldozer operators dressed in Sunday-best.

Not expecting a flow of rhetoric from such a man, I asked how he felt about building highways through the old neighborhoods, rooting up into old, beautiful valleys to build roads for subdivisions. Particularly, I asked, how did he feel bulldozing the home of some old Hawaiian family?

"Well," he smiled. "The Hawaiian in me, I feel sorry for the poor buggah. Then the Chinaman in me says, 'screw 'em'."

Suddenly you are looking through a hole in a contractor's fence at a new hole in the ground. Planners have hardly a moment to spare for preservation. They have all turned futurologist. Their world is a series of bar graphs, 1965, 1975, 1985, each more lofty and dizzying than the last. Each, years ahead of schedule, turns itself into a range of hotels, condominiums, and office buildings. When the lights go on here and there in the banked windows at dusk, the skyline takes on the formidable look of a deck of IBM cards punched to show the concentration and distribution of wealth.

Down on the streets of the city of leisure and delight, the big buildings block off the tradewinds and leave the palms in their lee standing still and faintly disconsolate. There is a man whose hobby it is to take the temperature of Kalakaua Avenue. It rises, it rises.

Atop the new $22-million office and bank complex, executive suites are teak-paneled and richly furnished. The offices and conference rooms exude influence, solidity and great wealth. Below in the harbor the white liner Lurline is at rest and tugs nudge other ships to waiting piers. Below, the cars move along Nimitz Highway, toy-sized.

The firm was founded a century ago by two missionary workers turned businessmen. They sold staples – cloth, hardware and tinned goods. Now the Company is listed on the New York Stock Exchange. It owns a pineapple cannery and a major island growing the fruit. It cans salmon in the Northwest, tuna at Kewalo Basin, manages endless miles of sugarcane, nurses great plantings of macadamia nuts. Its interests range from the Philippines to Alaska. It employs Aleuts, Hukbalahaps, Hawaiians and Hollanders. It has almost finished a planned community near Honolulu.

The new kamaaina moves here, directing, improving, expanding the interests of the old. The firm's president is a mainland Scot, long in the islands. *Twenty-five years ago, he headed a Community Chest campaign to raise some $150,000. Recently, the United Fund need was over $4 million and he sat on a committee that overshot the goal – serving with a union leader he has long fought bitterly. This is the shape of things and he knows it.*

The man at the other end of his telephone is at a Wall Street investment banking house. Another man waits outside to report on the company's large housing development in California. He hangs up the phone and walks with me to the door, and we pass a glass case displaying the antique account-books, pens and inkpots of the founders. He pauses and points out an error in bookkeeping:

"Maybe it was a mistake, but maybe the accountant stole fifty cents on the deal."

The artifacts are interesting. So is his reaction.

A good many local people who have seen Honolulu put on a concrete necklet to go with its coral find delight in the new adornment.

The old sugar companies have indeed diversified, and are now heavily involved in tourism. The trustees of the big landed estates of the chiefs' descendants are putting their sprawling properties to what is called "highest and best use."

For other locals, there are not many places in the world where the path from plantation village to penthouse has been so broad and so smooth. Any number of Oriental families have risen in three generations from the culture of sugarcane for subsistence to the cultivation of the condominium as an investment. For them, the more construction the better. The symbol of a long and happy life is still a thousand cranes.

Reinforcing steel for highrise hotel, Honolulu.

VII Directions

In his mid-fifties now, the haole union leader sits in his simple office as we talk. When younger, he was burly-tall and crawled through the canefields to secret meetings with men who were scared and needed reassurance. Now he is thinner, tired, recently fought off an illness. Long one of the most powerful men in the islands, he estimates seventy-five percent of his time goes into non-union matters.

"Battles aren't the same when you know you're going to win," he says. "I've got one or two fights left in me. But I can't find a place, or cause.

"We get nostalgic, remembering the old days, and we feel uncomfortable, having to be responsible. We can't pull down the temple because it's ours – a unique position for guys who used to fight the establishment. It was a lot easier to call the boss a dirty bastard.

"By and large, the young people are not interested in the standards set up by us. They don't give a damn about what happened twenty years ago. When we were young, we had something solid to punch. We were fighting a class enemy, or collaboration – even our own guys selling out for dollars and cents. Nowadays, they're swinging wild, and even at us. 'The unions are worse than the boss,' they say. The kids of our union members are the least understanding.

"I'd like to bring in one of these bright youngsters – get one into the organization. But the son of a bitch would probably turn on us . . ."

In his board room, the Chinese financier worries about many of the same things.

"I remember," he says, "how proud I was as a boy when my mother would take me visiting with her. We would dress in our best and walk down the street together. In my own family today, we still have Sunday dinner together, my wife and our three sons. But the communication is not there. Sometimes I feel the boys do not understand us at all. They have their own worlds and problems and our old memories and experiences mean nothing to them. I remind them that their grandparents came here in steerage in the 1890s. Almost three months on the water, with all the privations, dangers and sufferings. But now our third and fourth generations think like mainland haoles. They are no longer Chinese. 'That was a long time ago, Dad,' they say, and I can see they're bored.

"The family is not what it used to be. Nor are the races. Once we banded together for help, we needed each other. There were the old societies of people from the same villages in China or prefectures in Japan. But with time and affluence, all that has been splintered and shattered. The fragmentation came with the financial independence. So we go our ways."

With statehood, Hawaii marked another ending, another beginning. The war, in brutal, backhand fashion, opened up fine new possibilities for people. Far more happily, statehood did the same. Hawaii has been transformed twice in one generation.

For good or ill, insularity is gone. We live now in open, changeful, traveling times, and find ourselves going in many directions at once. We do business with all the world. We look searchingly at what comes up out of our soil, and at the skies and oceans that envelop us. We see more of other peoples' lives than ever, in peace and war, and they of ours. We grow and alter. And as we do, we are brought to consider how much of the outside world we want, what we do not want, how much we are committed to the past, and what we are willing to invest in a future of high promise but some uncertainty.

We find, to begin with, that we do not have much time for reflection. Things happen very fast nowadays. We have passed ourselves any number of times since 1959. Population is up more than twenty-five percent since statehood – more than fifty percent on Oahu. Property values have tripled – quadrupled on Oahu. Personal income is up one-third. Telephones have doubled, department store sales and university enrollments have increased 400 percent. Something like $4 billion worth of construction has been put in place. We are using vast quantities of sand, rock, and cinder for building, and are on the verge of running out of Hawaiian names for streets.

It sounds like the American dream: the works of nature steadily incorporated into the works of man, everything getting bigger, going ahead, everyone more prosperous, sociable, well-instructed all the time. The figures tell us so, and we are pleased to hear them.

The difficulty is that rapid growth produces other sets of figures as well, and these we must attend to. It costs more to live here than any place in the country (except, we hear, Anchorage, Alaska). State and local taxes are the highest in the nation. Food prices alarm, housing costs dismay. Each year Honolulu manufactures more crime, garbage, noise. The city puts about 450,000 tons of pollutant into the air every twelve months, and each inhabitant breathes in about thirteen-and-a-half pounds. Perspective ought to be maintained: the air of Los Angeles is something like eighty times worse. But we have always been privileged to think clean air is the only kind, and now we discover that in one small part of bustling Honolulu the lead count from car exhausts is almost as high as on the Hollywood Freeway, and ozone is killing lichens. Comparisons cannot help being odious. Still, thirteen-and-a-half pounds of pollutant seems enough. We will take suggestions for reducing it. The urban bad dream is something we surely do not want from the outside world.

"The population explosion has blown us out of touch with each other," an old friend said one night, in one of those conversations that have become so common.

"What I mean is that, like in 1955, everybody who was doing anything in town knew everybody else, at least by reputation or nodding acquaintance. Downtown, the business, law, political crowd gathered at Ciro's or M's Tavern or the Young Hotel every day for morning coffee or lunch. Now, you walk into a restaurant and they're mostly strangers. I don't mean visitors, I mean new guys in town who are doing things bigger than we were doing – much bigger – airline and manufacturing and banking and hotel guys. You see a few old friends, familiar faces, but that's about it. Not long ago you could walk up Bishop or along Merchant and say hello to every third man. Now everything is so hurried and we move among strangers – are strangers to each other.

"We've accepted it, are lost in it, caught up in the whole New Honolulu. It's a tidal wave you can't fight. We're taut, tense, up-tight with the affluence; it's a different world and we've become different with it. We no longer have time for each other. Even the amenities have deadlines. Once there were so many hours. Now it's moments between deals and deadlines and obligations.

"Let's say I haven't seen a man in a long time. Suddenly, he hustles by, preoccupied, hurrying through the beach crowds. Maybe I say hello. And ask how things are going – what is he doing these days? And the answer comes

something like, he put up an apartment building on the old place and it pays off pretty well. He and his wife have a home over on Maui and go there quite a bit. And howzit with me? And I tell him, and first thing you know we are only talking about how busy we are and shaking our heads. Almost always, we touch on The Good Old Days – ten years ago! – and maybe there's a laugh or two, but not the real funny laughs like before. And pretty soon we're looking over each other's shoulders . . ."

The gods dispense premonitions. Once in a great while, Kilauea in eruption covers all the islands with smoke clouds. This happened recently. The sky over Honolulu turned business grey and featureless. The mountains were erased, the city looked like a xerox copy of itself. People called the lowering stuff "vog," volcanic smog, and made wan jokes about it. In the half light, Honolulu had lost its garden.

What Kilauea does here, man himself has done already in other places not so far away. Traces of exhaust in the air are being picked up by scientists at Cape Kumukahi on the Big Island. The winds being what they are, these can only be coming from California. We should choose our directions with care.

Still, take it all in all, growing pains, cost of living, dead lichens, everything, Honolulu is very livable, especially by the standards of other city dwellers. They come, most of them, from grimmer parts. They do not look for urban delinquencies here, and they simply do not find them. Money is only money, after all, but sunshine is happiness and cannot be bought. Turn your head, and you can still see something beautiful here.

A few years ago some conservationists walked into Kipahulu valley, an out-of-the-way place on Maui, to see what was there. They started from the Seven Sacred Pools, a spot of Edenic beauty. They climbed more than 7,000 feet to an undisturbed stand of native koa trees, the finest in the islands, to a zone of ohia farther up, and at last to the cold crater rim of Haleakala.

They were all alone, and they could almost hear the singing silence of the turning earth. They saw in a clear stream the slender red damselfly mating. For them the scarlet iiwi bird plunged his long curved orange-red-pink bill into the perfectly receptive pink flower of a native lobelia, and not many people alive have seen that eloquent and elegant evolutionary display. One of the bird men netted some crested honeycreepers on a pelea tree and took them back, small branch and all, to his tent at night. He stuck the branch in his boot, and the birds flew to it and would not leave. They slept there. Next morning he got up early, and rather than shake them awake he went out barefoot. There is a virtue in being gentle with wilderness. In places like Kipahulu are the roots of heaven.

These careful men found four kinds of birds and several plants that everybody thought were extinct. If the expedition had so much as cut careless trails, they would have opened up the way for the destruction of native species by offering invaders a foothold.

With any luck Kipahulu will be left to itself. No one lives in the valley now although Charles Lindbergh, we hear, is going to settle there. This is appropriate. One old eagle in Kipahulu is enough.

To get away from Honolulu, traffic and confusion for a day or two, one good place to go is Molokai, which is more like the Hawaii-places of earlier days, unruffled and quiet. The town of Kaunakakai, for example, is near deserted in the afternoon and a stroller can visit all its stores, poke his head in all its poolrooms and bars, in less than two hours. It has changed very little in thirty years.

One afternoon I stopped at the bar of a little hotel there and overheard a conversation between the hotel manager and an old friend who was getting pleasantly tipsy as they recalled other days together.

The manager said, "I can sit here on the lanai and watch those planes going over the channel from Honolulu to Maui and the Big Island, passing us by. Not too many people ever heard of Molokai except for Father Damien and the leper colony. And you know what? Even if business is bad, I don't really give a goddam, because it's another world over here. I'm not starving and I'm through hustling . . . You can still leave your door unlocked here and trust your neighbor. There's no delinquency, the way there is in Honolulu, with screwballs writing dirty words on buildings and cars banging each other everywhere. People are still warm and trusting here and you're welcome everywhere. They'd be hurt, even insulted, if you didn't accept their giving and hospitality . . ."

The two stared out over the placid channel. The bulk of Maui island was dark and high over sun-sparkled water and hundreds of hidden mynahs chirped in a nearby banyan.

"Count your blessings," said the oldtimer. "They won't last long. The business will find you, even if you don't want it. And when it does, for God's sake be different. Repel it."

The liquor was warming him up and he grinned at his idea. "Forget this 'Molokai, The Friendly Island' crap. That's Mickey-Mouse stuff. Why not call it 'Molokai – The Savage Island?' Make it hard to get. The first tourist off the plane every morning is notified he won first prize. He will be the human sacrifice at nightfall. Get some guys to go up in the hills and beat on drums all night. Have some big Hawaiian walk through the lobby in a jockstrap every afternoon and when someone complains or asks who he is, you ask who? – Tell 'em you didn't see anything. Kill the pig for the luau on the front lawn at lunchtime so everybody can hear the screams and see the blood. Drive the tourists goofy with all sorts of spooky stuff . . ." He paused, looked back over the channel and laughed harshly.

"Only trouble with this, is that the way fads and fashions go nowadays, you might become a big success – become the 'in' place for the jet set."

Again, difficulties. The thing about untouched beauty is that people instantly want to touch it. For every one who comes to live in the islands we are to expect a hundred just looking. In the early 1970s the outer islands will have more hotel rooms for tourists than all of the Caribbean. Not too far ahead is the time when the mainland will be only three hours and a day's pay away for the average man. At that point we will surely become more than ever like other places. And it is our difference that is precious.

That is why we do so much arguing back and forth about tourism and its relation to society. Everyone has an opinion, and some perfectly responsible economists say tourism is indispensable to the islands, the biggest single item in the civilian economy.

The arguments go on. We have let the business grow too quickly; we should look for quality rather than quantity. We should zone for beauty, or at least for comfort, and not for speed, or the place will uglify

202

Left to right: Professor Arne Naess, University of Oslo,
Dr. Hajime Nakamura, University of Tokyo, and
Dr. Nadjm Bammate from UNESCO's Division of
Cultural Studies, Paris; East-West Philosophers Conference,
East-West Center, University of Hawaii, Oahu.

Left: Children, late afternoon, Waikiki Beach, Honolulu, Oahu.
Below: Dr. Wallace Gray, East-West Philosophers Conference on Alienation. East-West Center, University of Hawaii, Oahu.

itself out of desirability, and we will be left poor and blighted – double jeopardy. We should consider residents ahead of tourists, and make sure tourism pays for itself by putting on a head tax or a room tax. We should not do this at all, or even talk about it, for fear that the world will get the idea that we do not want tourists, and then no one will love us any more. We should not even consider limits or controls on tourism, because that would be a sorry withdrawal of the ultimate blessing the islands offer – the gift of generous welcome, in a spirit of aloha. We should forget all that, because the spirit of aloha is long dead, killed by progress. We are a bellhop society, smiling for tips.

We carry on like this all the time, accusing and defending ourselves, and the case always concerns what people will think of us, and what we should be able to think of ourselves. We look forward to the time when tourists will think $600 million a year of us, and then we worry about what is being bought and sold. If tourism should fail, it will certainly mean economic disaster. If tourism should ever come to dominate the economy altogether, that might be a disaster of a more subtle kind. Nobody – resident or tourist – could really want Hawaii to settle for life as a ten-cent postcard.

The pool and beach at the Kahala Hilton is like Beverly Hills West. The movie stars and producers and corporate executives sit, sip, soak sun and plan the chess moves that will be relayed on wires or murmured on phones later to New York or Hollywood.

Bobby the beachboy does brisk business in surfboards, beachchairs, towels and lotion. Bobby used to work at Waikiki in the old days, taking the tourists out on boards

himself. Now he's an executive too and has two or three assistants. Bobby doesn't smile as much as he used to. He has that looking-over-your-shoulder thing going. He talks at you pleasantly enough, but it's obvious he's in constant worry that someone important is not being taken care of. Does Jack Lord have the patch of shade he likes? Are Lennie Freeman's kids staying in shallow water? Is the volleyball court clear for Lawford and Sammy Davis?

The playboy publisher sits in the sun with his retinue of valet, finance and editorial men and pin-up companion. The publisher has just discovered Hawaii and likes it. His friends murmur facts and figures and he nods, absently. The gatefold girl anoints his pink shoulders with oil and croons in his ear and he smiles, sipping cola.

A part of the hotel sits astride a lagoon where three porpoises laze, their heads and snouts breaking the surface, blowholes spouting little puffs of vapor. At feeding time, David the trainer, puts them through their paces from a small platform and the crowd gathers to watch the animals jumping, flapping, doing the hula wearing plastic leis, leaping through hoops and tossing a rubber ball back and forth. Cameras click and whir. The animals obey every clang of the trainer's bell, every command he voices. They race through the water for their reward-herring.

Tourism was encouraged after the war for the simplest of reasons – Hawaii had nothing much to sell except sugar and pineapple, and both crops had problems. They still do. Not that they cannot be grown efficiently here. The two local industries are world leaders in the kind of scientific research that leads to high productivity. But they are bedeviled by high costs – or, more exactly, low costs elsewhere. Pineapple, in particular, can be grown in other places where labor is much cheaper. The crop is still worth $130 million to the islands, but Hawaii's share of the world market in canned pineapple has gone down in the last twenty years from seventy-two percent to forty-two percent, and there are people who think they can see the day coming when it might be phased out of the islands' altogether. This is already beginning to happen on Kauai, and people there are looking to tourism to take up the slack, which gives arguments about general welfare a sharp edge indeed.

The case of sugar is rather different. The U.S. market is closely regulated, and Hawaii has a quota, like any other producer. The Hawaiian Sugar Planters' Association does not look to going out of business, nor to spectacular growth on the order of tourism. Sugar will hold its own, perhaps do a little better than that, though local conditions will change. Prime sugar land will be re-zoned for urban use, especially on Oahu. Field laborers will be harder and harder to find, and all sorts of functions mechanized, even computerized.

Whatever happens, the Association's research scientists will go on looking for better varieties of cane. Their work has already led them past conventional breeding by pollination to experiments with the single sugarcane cell. They are able to take a cell and grow a complete plant from it. And because the canes they use are hybrids, "chromosomal mosaics," they get a wide variety of results. They look forward to manipulating the single cell further. They propose to strip the walls from cells with enzymes and fuse them. Or to dose a single cell with nucleic acid to induce favorable characteristics. All this is prophecy, but prophecy being worked out in test tubes and evidently not far from fulfillment. Which is to say that new plants will be produced, plants impossible to produce by traditional breeding, plants never seen before.

These researchers work close to the source of things. Man cannot do without the green plant. The plant puts the sun to work, and here are men putting the plant itself to work more subtly than before, bypassing evolution, playing with time, breaking down and recombining the elements of life, rearranging the future. They are enlargers of our experience.

The firms that have always controlled sugar and pineapple here, the Big Five, used to be famous for their exclusivity and provinciality. No more. Since statehood, they have enlarged their own experience. They continue to grow their two staple crops here, but elsewhere as well. They also go into land development, acquire subsidiaries, make operating agreements with the biggest money men in the world, offer their shares on the Big Board, and get their names on lists of the largest firms in the country.

Amfac Inc. has operations on four continents. Castle & Cooke works in three Latin American and five Asian countries. C. Brewer & Co. is building sugar plantations in Iran and Iraq and training management men and technologists in Ecuador, Colombia, and Taiwan. Theo. H. Davies & Co. makes television sets in the Philippines and air-conditioners in Spain. The Big Sixth, the Dillingham Corporation, does business all over the Pacific Basin.

The financial world of the big firms expands all the time. Alexander & Baldwin has headquarters in Honolulu, but finds that most of its money decisions

Below: Prism reflectors, laser beam geodimeter,
Volcano Observatory, Island of Hawaii.

Opposite: Geochemist taking fresh lava sample
near Kilauea Crater, Island of Hawaii.

Below: Papaya irradiation, wholesomeness and
ripening study, Hawaii Research Irradiator,
University of Hawaii.
Right: U.S. Department of Agriculture
fruit fly research program, Honolulu.

are taken where the money is, on the mainland, and that will be more and more true from now on. Money flows two ways. More than a thousand mainland firms, half of them California-based, do business here. Points of origin make less and less difference.

The little bars are numerous and near-secret. Most are windowless, many are on side streets, shielded by hedges or fences, identified only by Japanese names on modest signs. Inside all are dark and space is divided into highbacked booths.

Few open until midafternoon. The customers trickle in quietly, almost formally, singly or in small groups. The clientele is overwhelmingly Oriental and completely male. Many are in business, politics, law and the professions. A few are blue-collar men, builders, craftsmen – fresh-scrubbed.

As the arrivals pause, adjusting eyes to the gloom and selecting their booths, the platoon of waitresses eases out to work. Almost all the girls are Japan-Japanese, imported solely for service in these sotto-voce spas. The girls wear no uniforms, and are all quite pretty. Most speak only a few words of English but little is required. Their job is femininity, obeisance, saying yes, yes, yes; exuding joy at being allowed to sit close to the men, admiring, leaping to service when needed. They bow, smile constantly, bring little dishes of pickled vegetables or meat and fish bits with drinks. They know when to touch a man's arm with affection and when to nod discreet, understanding smiles as he discusses business with companions.

Most of the patrons have never been to Japan, and speak but a few words of Japanese. Yet it is pleasant at the end of a long day to sit in cool gloom with a beautiful girl and sip a drink with friends. Or simply to be alone and fawned upon by the brief-skirted 1970 Geishas.

There are no illusions about the service. When it is time to go men leave a tip, say goodnights and walk to their cars. They drive home to substantial houses in broad-lawned subdivisions, where there are bicycles in the driveway, wives in the kitchen with their problems and children to be chided. After dinner they browse through the "Star-Bulletin" before it's time for "Hawaii Five-O" on TV.

Business will make its way whether sugar and pineapple thrive or not. There is even some talk about a rather specialized new business fortune to be made from the sea. The oceangoing trade here amounts to the handling of six million tons of cargo a year, worth $850 million. But the trade that sails by Honolulu without stopping amounts to fifty-five million tons of cargo worth $9 billion. This argues for making Honolulu a great oceanic freightyard.

International shipping has always operated in a tangle of competing union jurisdictions, national laws, trade agreements, and cargohandling procedures. Matson Navigation Co., owned by Alexander & Baldwin, has led the way in making sense out of one part of this tangle: the way cargo gets on and off ships. They use huge boxes, called containers, and they have speeded the turnaround of their ships enormously. It is one big step from this to have all shipping lines go to containers, and another far more adventurous one to having containers shipped, trucked and taken by rail in an uninterrupted stream linking Asia with America and Europe, with Honolulu as a major transfer point. The idea has been around for some time, and the problems are great. But it is as important as anything that is being considered in modern shipping, and someday it may make Hawaii a lot of new money, and do the world some practical good. It already has a resonant name – International Intermodality.

Another thing which has always made a great deal of money for Hawaii is war – War and Cold War. That is to say, Defense. The biggest single item in the state's economy is military spending. At $600 million a year and rising (up eighty-five percent since 1959), it is one-third again as big as tourism, and far bigger than sugar and pineapple together. One person out of every seven or eight in the islands is a serviceman or a serviceman's wife or child. CINCPAC, Commander-in-Chief, Pacific, has his headquarters at Pearl Harbor. His domain covers forty percent of the globe, and he has a million men and women in uniform.

This is a considerable military presence, as the phrase goes. Yet somehow Honolulu manages not to look like a garrison town, even with Pearl Harbor and Hickam Air Force Base and Schofield Barracks just down the road – though we do see the GIs making their weekend reconnaissances of Hotel Street and Kalakaua Avenue, and the men from Vietnam on rest and recuperation leave, hundreds of thousands of them over the years.

About all the professional activity observable in the islands we are somewhat ambivalent, particularly following the news that we are being considered as a site for anti-missile missiles, presumably because other people already have us in mind as a missile target. Polaris submarines slide in and out of Pearl Harbor. Aircraft carriers loom past Barbers Point. Jets of one sort or another are up most of the time. The anti-submarine warfare test range at Barking Sands on Kauai picks up noises on its hydrophones. And here and there on high places you come across the unearthly dome of a tracking station, looking like the helmet of some prodigious Hawaiian warrior in the hills.

The Navy bombs Kahoolawe again. This time they drop a 500-pounder on Maui, another island altogether. It hits – of all places – some pastureland leased by the mayor. It does not explode, but the mayor is not visibly amused.

Down in the forest reserve at Waiakea on the Big Island something stirs. It turns out, under persistent questioning by Hawaii's congressmen, to be the Army, testing nerve gas, seven miles from the nearest civilians, fourteen from the large town of Hilo. The governor was not told about the tests. Neither was the state's Department of Land and Natural Resources, which drew up the lease for the Army. On this matter too we are ambivalent.

And about the fact that the Atomic Energy Commission explodes atom bombs underground in the Aleutians, on the unstable rim of the Pacific. This is where our biggest tsunamis, oceanic shock waves, come from already. Sometimes they kill people.

If peace should ever break out, Hawaii will certainly lose some money. This time it is a question of what the whole world is buying and selling.

The papers said the Apollo spaceship would only be visible from Hawaii that morning, that the weather would be overcast, so there wasn't much hope of seeing it.

But I awoke early, before dawn, and went out and looked skyward. I saw star-sparklings, so I got binoculars and went out on the beach. There is a point of land jutting out in front

214

Pacific Submersibles' research vehicle, Naia,
at Makai Test Range, Oahu.

of the Kahala Hilton next door and I stumbled out there in the dark. There were only a few lights in our apartment building and even fewer in the hotel. The world was asleep. The sky above was quite clear. The faintest hint of dawn outlined a low mountain-cloud on the eastern horizon.

At first, the spaceship was indistinguishable from stars low in the western sky. Then it became larger, moving out in a grand, long sweep over the southern horizon. Its glow heightened, burning bright, not a star but an eerie, glorious man-thing. My back prickled at the wonder of it. Like an arrow flying into infinity, it threw off fan-shaped rays above, below and behind, facet-gleamings of a diamond.

There were probably only a few hundred people in all the world witnessing this wonder – and I was one of them, feeling tremendously small and alone. The earth – all things – had grown smaller in those few moments.

And so it traveled, sure and strong, lighting the sky for a few minutes in a gentle arc over the Southern Cross. The men inside had already ignited it and that was why it was so sharp and easy to see. It went behind the low clouds for a few moments and was out of sight. But the glow remained, outlining the clouds. Then it reappeared and there was a flash. It was then that it took off for the moon.

I thought of the three men inside, headed for the moon at 24,000 miles an hour, and I wondered if they had time for thoughts – for a glance perhaps at the night lights of Honolulu and the islands below.

The man-star faded as it had flamed, slowly, slowly to be lost back among the other specks in dark sky.

I walked back to the apartment. It had all taken but a few minutes. The beach and the buildings were still dark, empty and silent. It was as if nothing had happened. Nothing had changed, and yet everything had changed.

About men on the moon there is less ambivalence and more natural awe, though Hawaii is actually quite conversant with space. Astronauts do their training for moonwalking in the volcanic craters here, where the earth is like the lunar surface. For the Apollo 11 moon shot, the National Aeronautics and Space Administration had its switching center at Honolulu. Kokee tracking station on Kauai had 115 technicians at work. Palehua Air Force Observatory near Barbers Point, and the Mees Solar Observatory of the University of Hawaii on Haleakala were keeping watch for solar flares, disturbances which give out showers of particles that might kill an astronaut if he were caught out walking in just his space suit.

After Armstrong, Aldrin, and Collins came back from their journey, the better part of a million miles including orbits, they splashed down in the central Pacific, precisely 912 miles southwest of Honolulu, and were brought on an aircraft carrier to Pearl Harbor. President Nixon waved at them through their window, and Armstrong played his ukulele for the world. But the astronauts did not actually set foot here, being quarantined for transshipment to Houston in their own special container.

The seismometer left on the moon by the astronauts to measure lunar quakes and other disturbances was thought up and partly designed by George Sutton of the University of Hawaii's Institute of Geophysics. Another enlarger of our experience. Science will not let us be insular any more.

At the same time, Sanford Siegel, a university botanist, is doing exobiology, the study of organic life on other planets – from earth, of course. The environment of Mars has been simulated in the laboratory – lack of oxygen, hardly any water, terrible cold – and some earthly plants have survived, and simple forms like molds have reproduced themselves. Siegel thinks that short of everything burning up, some form of life can survive any stressful condition. This is probably useful knowledge for the twentieth century.

He was one of the few haoles working the beach for one of the big hotels and I remember seeing him there often before the war. If a man can be called beautiful, this guy was it – he was tall, magnificently muscled and tanned, had teeth that gleamed, fine, sharp features and a Byronesque head of hair. All of us ordinary guys were jealous of him. Women were mad about him, wouldn't leave him alone. Yet he was a quiet sort, shy and serious.

He was a marvelous water-man, surfing, canoeing and swimming. Once, he rode and paddled a surfboard all the way to Kauai, over rough stormy open sea, and there were big newspaper stories about it. When the war came and the beach closed down all the beachboys got jobs at Pearl or Hickam or other defense installations and I think that was when he went on the police force. He got married about that time too, to a nice looking, but not spectacular girl. She was a nurse or something like that. The reason I remember is because everyone supposed he'd easily grab some millionaire's daughter or rich woman off the beach.

I don't know when or how he cracked up. Years passed. Maybe he was in Kaneohe Hospital. I don't know. But for the last nine or ten years, I've seen him quite often, as many as three-four times a week.

He's like a skeleton now, wears tattered, grimy clothes and beatup sneakers, pants pockets bulging with God knows what. He has no teeth, his hair is long and scraggly.

And he walks. That's all he does, walk, walk, walk. Most often, I see him on Diamond Head Road, or along Kapiolani Park or the Ala Wai. He seems to stay away from more crowded places. He just strides as if going some-place, with his head down, looking at his feet, never stopping. One of the oldtime cops said he lives in a cave somewhere on Diamond Head.

Once I passed him and stopped the car on impulse.

"Bricky? You're Bricky, aren't you?" He stopped as if scared. Looking at him it was impossible to imagine the gold god in swim tights of years ago. His skull was a death's head. He squinted at me. And he moved back a step.

"I'm Sheehan," I told him. "You gave me some surf lessons once . . . Way back. Remember?"

He answered in a whisper. "Yes, Mr. Sheehan. I remember." I knew he didn't.

"How are things going, Bricky?" It was the only thing I could think to say and it sounded so foolish.

"Everything's fine, Mr. Sheehan," he mumbled.

"Anything I can do for you, Bricky?"

"No. Nothing . . . Thanks anyway."

He put his head down and walked on, faster.

Sometimes modernity seems to be a mostly stressful condition. We are all in it together. The military has a communications satellite arrangement called SAT-COM, civilians have one called COMSAT. Both have ground stations in Hawaii, and COMSAT's, at Pau-malu on Oahu, is the biggest of its kind in the world. It is new, it has been blessed, and one of its major uses has been to pick up war pictures from Vietnam and beam them to its slave stations. And of course

Above: Porpoise in training tank, Oceanic Institute, Oahu.

Right: Oceanic Institute's plexi-glass hulled submersible, Kumu, during test dive, Bateson's Bay, Oahu.

Right: Kumu test crew, builder and test pilot Bill Walker on right. Bateson's Bay, Oahu.

Overleaf left: Makai Range's Habitat II, Aegir, in tow to dive site, Waimanalo Bay, Oahu.

Overleaf right: Habitat II flooding ballast and submerging, Waimanalo Bay.

Right: Habitat II engineer observing test dive,
Waimanalo Bay, Oahu.
Far right: Habitat II on bottom, test dive, Waimanalo Bay.

Left: Plastic seagrass, algae-growing experiment,
Bateson's Bay, Oceanic Institute, Oahu
Below: Diver with plastic seagrass, Bateson's Bay.

CINCPAC maintains his constant surveillance of two-fifths of the world.

In the sea as well a great deal of information-passing and interrogation goes on. Hawaii has obvious advantages as a center for oceanographic studies, and has become the first state to consider a plan for development of the ocean, intellectual and industrial, a plan that could bring the islands $250 million annually in research and resources by the end of the century.

In the meantime, out of self-interest as much as scientific passion, Hawaii has become the leading place for research on tsunamis, and is in communication with recording stations all around the Pacific. The University's Institute of Geophysics sends out research vessels that bring back useful information on everything from wave formation to the mysteries of continental drift. One marine laboratory lowers a camera 4,500 feet into the water, and gets photographs of some very strange creatures indeed. Another puts men in an environment that simulates conditions of great underwater pressure, and finds (among many interesting things) that they become obstreperous and their voices go squeaky. Experience is enlarged in strange ways.

The privately financed Makapuu Oceanic Center on windward Oahu has a comprehensive interest in what happens when we who evolved out of the water go back in. The Center is an educational marine exhibit, Sea Life Park; a marine research facility, The Oceanic Institute; and The Makai Test Range, concerned with marine engineering. A set of sophisticated steel tanks called Habitat II, designed at the Makai Range, gives men a way to live at the ocean floor for up to three weeks, with access to the sea outside and electronic contact with the surface.

The Institute is getting ready for something like a submarine moon shot – an encapsulated journey under the sea, from Hawaii to California. Three men will go, probably in 1971, in a vessel called Deep Voyager, whose most important structural parts are made, improbably, from glass. A glass sphere conforms to pressure rather than resisting it, and so gets stronger and stronger at depth. Accordingly, the three deep voyagers will ride in an eighty-four-inch sphere linked in a hull to two more spheres containing their life support systems. They will proceed in elegant simplicity, with only the smallest of engines. They will make fifty passes through a glide cycle of fifty miles, from the surface down to 20,000 feet and up again. The downward glide starts with the flooding of water tanks, and at the bottom of the cycle a hydrazine fuel generates enough buoyancy to get Deep Voyager to rise again. They will reach San Diego in sixteen days, and on the way they will see things no one has ever seen.

Another of the Institute's current interests is getting nourishment from the sea for an overpopulated earth. By and large, twentieth-century man on the ocean has been like old-stone-age man on the land, a hunter and gatherer, following his food, not knowing enough to farm it. The Hawaiian learned to do better than that, with walled fishponds of brackish water along the shore. Several years ago the Institute got involved in bringing some ponds on Molokai back into production. The idea was that if mullet and milkfish could be bred and harvested in Hawaii, the same thing could eventually be done wherever these fish are known, and there would be a useful dividend of protein for the tropical world, which is generally protein-poor.

The Molokai ponds still had their walls, and there were still Hawaiians who knew some of the things that used to be done, though they were not doing them any more. Working along good research lines, the Institute scientists established the salinity and temperature of the water needed for breeding, and a number of other essentials. And as they went back and forth between pond and laboratory they discovered something else as well: they were doing over again what the Hawaiian had done for himself.

The native knew that the exact saltiness of the water had a lot to do with what happened, and so they placed their walled ponds where rain water from the hills would go around the ends and not through the middle. They knew that one set of things would happen if the walls were permeable, another if they were not. They had a system of gates and tidal checks to keep predators out. They knew that the fish needed a deep spot to survive. They used to work, a village of people all together, scooping the pond bottoms clean with coconut shells, to keep the water right for the mullet.

And this, in the end, was why the ponds went out of production. The villages were pulled out of shape by haole society, and the Hawaiians were no longer able to do the things in common that made the fishponds work. The Institute scientists say that their experiments have at last got them to about where the Hawaiians used to be. They will be able to go on from there.

One of the Oceanic Center researchers has come to have a high regard for the way the Hawaiians did things. He says, more than half-seriously, that the land and sea of the islands ought to be put back under the control of local communities, with new kapus and new kahunas. The thought, not strictly professional and all the better for it, is that progress might be healthier with a graft to the roots of heaven.

He has a point. Not far from the Center is Kaneohe Bay, a nice place to swim and sail and generally get wet. A good many people prefer to live on the windward side of Oahu rather than in Honolulu, and Kaneohe keeps growing. One of the best times of year there is the clam season. Thousands of people like nothing better than to spend a day or two up to their knees in the warm waters of the bay, just clamming. But now that the inland hills are being developed for housing, the storm drains run millions of gallons of fresh water down to the bay. It is killing the clams. They are all but dead. There was no 1969 season. And in all the genuine simple disappointment over this, it turned out as well that the bay, a nice place to live, with new people moving in every day, is polluted, so much so that it is dying several hundred years ahead of its time.

None of this is anybody's fault, particularly – it is just the way we do things. It is easy to see how knowledge of land and ocean goes out of fashion. It is harder to see exactly where wisdom lies.

I have a friend who has great love for things Hawaiian. All his life he has known Hawaiians and feels their mystique with great sympathy. And all his life he has collected Hawaiiana—stone adzes, bowls, ancient implements like bone fishhooks and carrying gourds, akuas, the curiously shaped gods of households, stone poi pounders, coral files and needles and many other fascinating objects. His house is a small museum.

We camped once together in a place called Kapua, deep down on the Kona Coast, far away from the world, and walked for miles around the deserted old heiaus, the flat stone temples of long ago, the village sites, the grave mounds and the thin ribbons of smooth stone trails. There is an old holua there, a sled slide looking like a piece of cinder highway placed on a hillside. In past days the Hawaiians made sleds, covered the slope with ti leaves and raced down the incline on the green slickness. Standing there, it was not hard to imagine the gala in the sun, the shouts and laughs and cheers, the color of feathered capes and gleaming brown bodies. Now it is a stillness place, only the sea moves and sparkles.

We found a small cave, hidden under a kiawe thicket under the sharp drop of the holua. We squatted on its cinder floor, enjoying its shade. Then we started scraping in the earth among the seashells and twigs, looking for bone fish hooks or ulumaika, the smoothshaped small stone discs the Hawaiians used for their bowling games. Finding nothing, my friend started examining the walls. Suddenly he said, as if knowing, "I think it's up here."

He reached over my head and pulled dry dirt and stones from a tiny recess. Magically, he brought forth a long poi-pounder shaped piece of stone, about nine inches long and perfectly formed. "This is a good one," he said, "a very unusual shape."

We walked back along the beach to our camp for dusk was falling. We passed a rotting canoe, forlorn in the long rays of the sun, half-hidden in the tall grass.

Back in camp, we built a fire for supper and my friend washed the stone clean. He said he had a curious feeling about his find. It was not an ordinary pounder, he said. More likely it was a kahuna pestle, used by the priests for grinding medicine or potions. "I have an odd feeling about this stone," he said. "I think it has mana. I can feel its mana." Before we slept he carefully placed the stone on a box near our bedrolls.

In the morning it had disappeared. We scoured the area, looking everywhere, but it was gone.

And we were the only humans for many miles.

Perhaps the Hawaiian past has something to say to us, after all, if we will listen. Parts of the past are stored in the Bishop Museum at Honolulu, in air-conditioned rooms, on paper, on film, on magnetic tape, and there is a whole collection of chants recorded some decades ago on wax cylinders. The kahus have more of it, and will keep it to themselves. More again is buried, and the archeologists who set about to dig it up are like the fishpond scientists again, painfully finding out what the Hawaiians knew and hoping that something interesting and enlarging will emerge.

At a place not many people have heard of called Lapakahi, on the west coast of the Big Island, a whole Hawaiian village system, from uplands to ocean, has been located. No one has lived there since early this century, and no one really knows how long the Hawaiians lived there before that.

The apparatus of archeology is wildly varied here: light planes and helicopters for site surveys and infrared photogrammetry, fine brushes and tweezers for close work in the diggings, a copy of the *Bottle Collectors' Guide* for help with the later Hawaiian's drinking habits, and a subscription to a splendid monomaniacs' magazine called *Just Buttons*, for help on what he fancied in trousers. And a direct electronic link from the ramshackle hotel where the diggers bunk to a

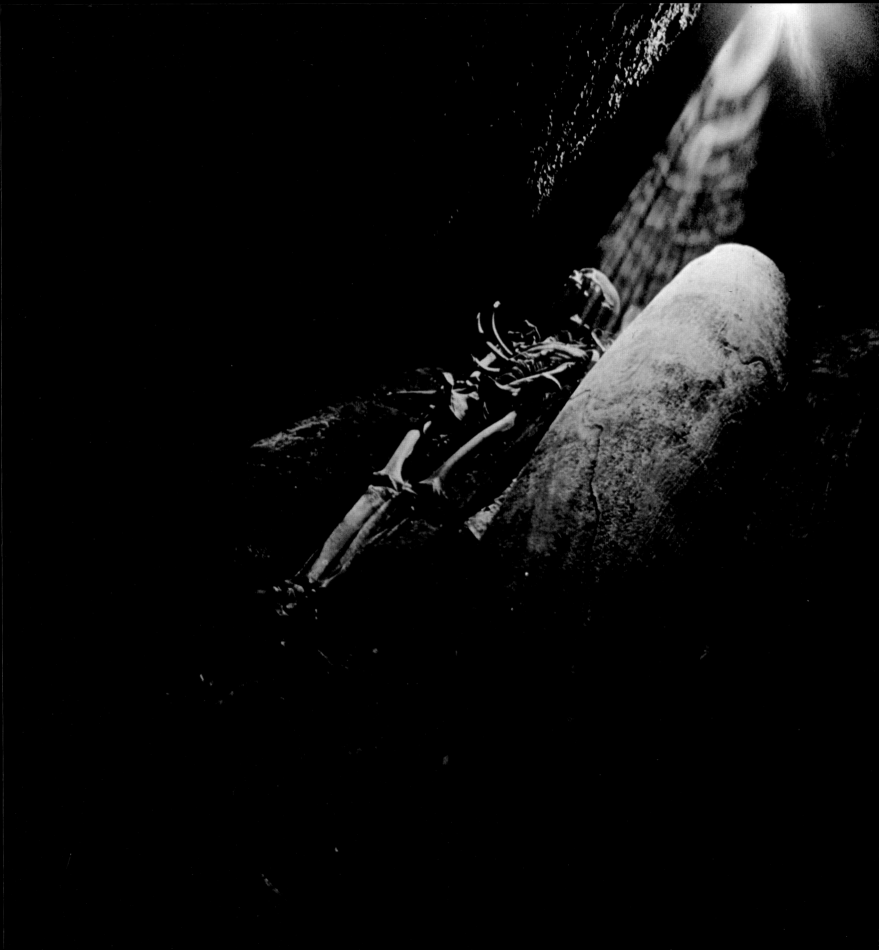

Below: Drawing of restoration plan,
Kaneaki Heiau, Makaha Valley, Oahu.

Right: Supply helicopter for archaeologists,
Keahole, Island of Hawaii.

Kaneaki Heiau, Makaha

entrance steps

computer, which receives information on each day's finds and suggests what might be important.

And what might be important? That Lapakahi was no paradise, but hot, rocky, and waterless, covered the last hundred years with the introduced algeroba, an obstinate, ugly, spiky tree whose thorns are everywhere to step on? Or that if the computer is right about fish-bone fragments, the Hawaiians did not seem to go out beyond the reef very much? That the skeleton discovered buried in half a dugout canoe is just bones to begin with, but when the skull is brushed off and the sightless eyes see the sun – suddenly, when the tobacco pipe with its teeth marks turns up, a person, a person?

One hot cloudy day at Lapakahi, a hundred degrees or more, absolutely still, with the stone-gray bowl of the sky pressing down, not a murmur in the kiawes, the air hanging on the skin like a heavy cloak, one of the diggers swung his pickaxe at the ground where nothing was supposed to be, and struck a skull and smashed it to smithereens. And a high awful wind rushed up out of nowhere and screamed through the valley and died again in an instant.

"I can't honestly say I'm ecstatic about the new Honolulu," the oldtimer was saying, "but the truth is, it's partly my doing, like the rest of us who have fed, fattened and grown on it. Face it squarely and we come up hypocrites. There are gnawings of regret and we wonder what we've done to ourselves. Yet we move in it, defend it, pretend the idyll, pay for the international rhapsodies of the Visitors Bureau – then go home to our fine apartments or houses on valley walls – our own personal little islands, untouched, safe and miles away from the rattle and hustle. We shut it out with walls of books, curtains of greenery and picture-windows on hillsides specially selected so others can't build and obstruct the view . . . and we curse the traffic and blame the politicians, developers and airlines. Yet we enjoy the profits, insulate ourselves, thinking: 'For myself, I'll keep things the way they used to be.'

"And we say, 'The Neighbor Islands. We must protect the Neighbor Islands; not make the same mistakes, not create other Waikikis – keep them unspoiled and beautiful, the way it was here on Oahu before the War.' But this is only talk. We do nothing because it doesn't really touch us. We only make mumbles about esthetics and planning."

Westerners, as Gregory Bateson of the Oceanic Institute says, have specialized in living at the front of the brain and have not paid enough attention to the back. The West has always put great stock in common sense – call it purposive consciousness, as Bateson does – without realizing that too much common sense, unredeemed, is bad for humanity. It may be efficient in the short run. But in the last hundred years, common sense has got the better of the environment, and this has made the long run look shorter. Now consciously purposive man, with the best of consciously purposive intentions, is capable of wrecking his environment and himself.

Bateson, another scientist with a care for the whole man, notes that there are some redeeming things that live at the back of the brain: dreams, religion, art. The question is whether the twentieth century is smashing them with a pickaxe.

In the islands as elsewhere, any number of artists

show us a future of fragments. Others try in their own way to heal. Joe Hadley takes castings in plaster directly from the naked human figure, grouping young men and women together and working at speed to set a fluid moment of grace before time gets away from him and his technology hardens everything over. He is telling us that art is brief, life long. Jerome Wallace works in seclusion at Anahola on Kauai, taking dyes for his batik paintings from barks and berries and lichens and the earth itself, as knowledgeably and frugally as any Hawaiian ever did. He lives alone, and sells his work all over the world.

Ed Stasack has taken to looking at petroglyphs, trying to understand what they say. The little figures chipped into rock all over the islands look simple, then turn complex, and finally cryptic in their admissions and omissions. They may be saying no more than that travelers passed this way and made a mark. Stasack finds it important that almost none of them show anything destructive being done. He takes molds of them and works them into wall panels for underpasses gouged into commercial streets in the city, stanching the urban wound with art. Not enough people stop to see what he has done. Again it is a question of what we buy and sell. Hawaii is exceptional in that, by law, the budget for all publicly built structures contains an appropriation for art. We are exceptional, and the figure is one percent.

There is an articulate man in the islands who talks about art and whistling winds. He is a champion surfer, and he finds that the waves bring things together for him, the front and the back of the mind. He is young, and has been in and out of society and its conventional states of consciousness. He talks well and thoughtfully, without thinking that words convey the quality of experience: words are fragments, experience is a wholeness, lived in real time. So when he is pressed to explain himself, he speaks of other things, widely separated things: physics and wave motion, the conscious direction of energy to the fingertips, adrenalin, Taoist philosophy. For an advanced surfer, he says, going into a wave is no longer just a drop and a turn. Now, he can see the same action as differing degrees of bite as his board goes down an ever-changing wave face. He uses differing weight positionings to get increasing speed, thrust, and gravitational pull. What he is doing, he says, is perceiving the wave in smaller and smaller units, because his mind has sharpened or speeded up and the wave has slowed down in relation to it. And in the end all this fractioning of experience makes the whole experience better. He is a particle in the wave. They flow together. He does not have to fight nature. He is on his way to becoming a whole man. He can do a 360-degree turn on a surfboard. Think about that – a full circle, coming down a wave . . .

"*When I was a youngster in Lahaina we had a wonderful life," Bill Brooks says. "Caleb Burns had a boat with an aquaplane and we used to go out in the morning and race over water oil-smooth and glassy. Sometimes we would aquaplane halfway to Lanai, far, far out. I will never forget how it was to be speeding over the water with the mountains behind, racing with the flying fish that scattered and flew ahead. The water was so clear you could see the bottom down fifty feet . . .*

"*I used to tie a string to my big toe when I went to bed*

Below right: Collecting lichen growth for dye.
Below left: Applying the dye to near-finished painting.
Opposite: Painter Jerome Wallace washing excess dye
from batik, near Waipahe'e, Kauai.

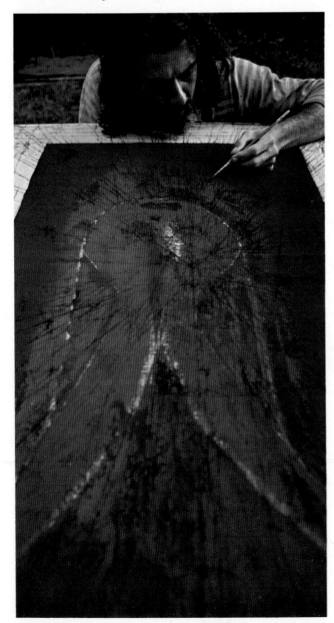

Left: Artist Ed Stasack preparing petroglyph form for mural
casting, in his studio, Honolulu.

Below: Making rubber mold of petroglyph from
Anaehoomalu, Kona Coast, Island of Hawaii.

238

Below left: Electrically separated Isoenzymes (proteins) from sugar cane leaves, research programs, Hawaiian Sugar Planters' Association, Honolulu.

Bottom: Photo–micrograph sugar crystals under polarized light, Experiment Station, HSPA.

Right: Artificial eclipse of the sun, green line corona, Mees Solar Observatory, Haleakala, Maui.

Far right: Micrograph, single sugar cell with chromosomes, HSPA research program.

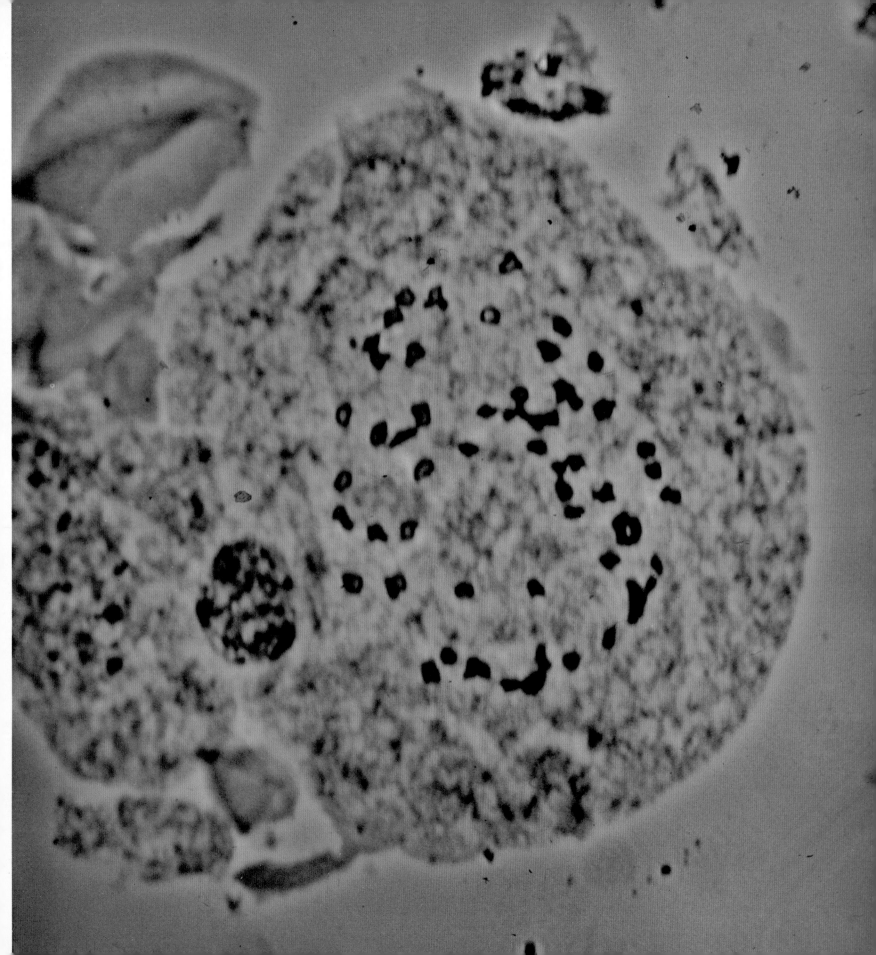

Below: Hydrogen cloud erupting from sun's surface,
coronagraph observation, Mees Solar Observatory,
Haleakala, Maui.

Right: Spectra of small flare on surface of sun.
Mees Solar Observatory, Haleakala.

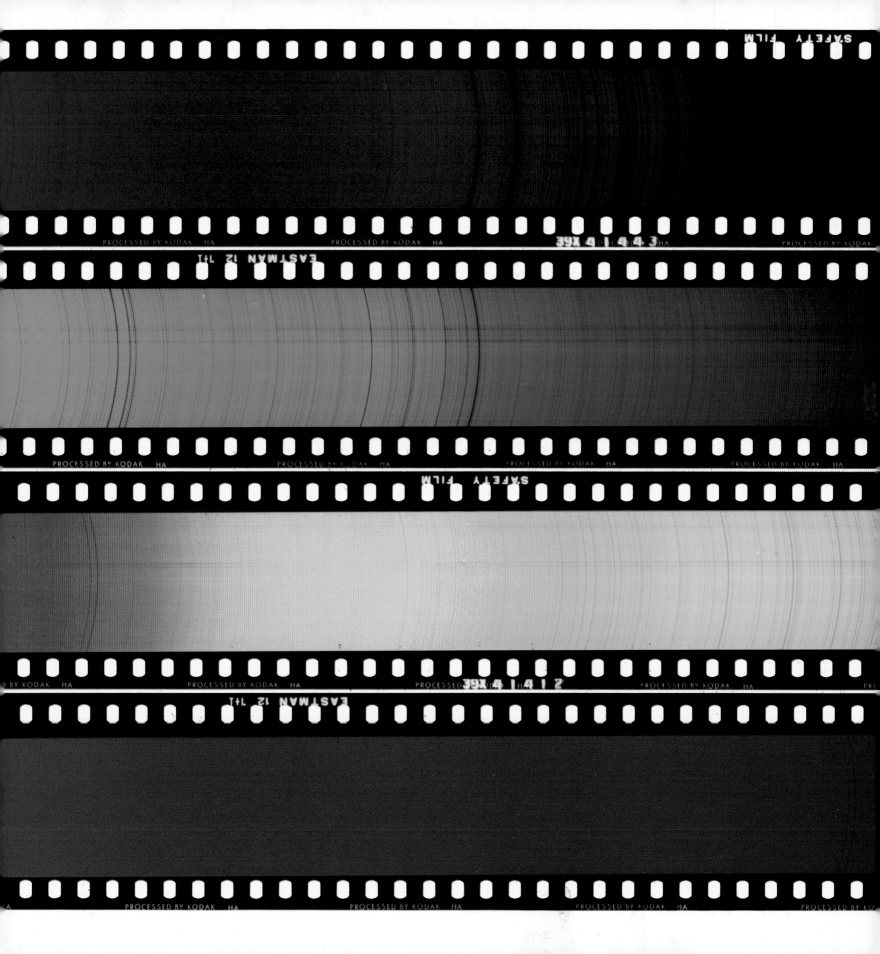

and hang the string out the window. When Buddy Farden's father got up to go to work, Buddy would get up, too, and come over and yank the string. Then we would go out in the dark and watch the big, beautiful fires as they burned off the sugarcane. When we went home afterwards for breakfast, it would still be dark."

Bill Brooks still has land in Lahaina and plans to build a hotel there. "There are others," Bill says, "who were kids in Lahaina with me who want to build big, tall ugly concrete highrises. I can't understand them. They don't need the money. Why do they want to ruin a place that still has so much of the old beauty?

"I want to build a hotel that has the oldtime flavor and graciousness – low buildings and beautiful plantings. And when it's finished I'm gonna take a shotgun and shoot it full of holes so it'll look right – like the termites have been at it."

Haleakala, where Hawaiian paniolos still surf the land, is the great mountain of Maui. The winding road to the top takes you through the cloud layer to an earth of volcanic rock and a sky of clear and bitingly cold air. At the summit, put your thumb up and cover the sun, and you can see clear blue sky all the way to your thumbnail. Astronomers call this good seeing. There is less of it in the world than there used to be. The biggest telescopes on the mainland are compromised by smog. For the time being, Hawaii has an exceptionally clear window on the universe.

Haleakala – and Mauna Kea on the Big Island – were made for astronomy, so astronomers say. Both mountaintops have observatories. The one on Mauna Kea is the highest spot in the Pacific. It does nighttime work. Haleakala concentrates on solar observation.

This is appropriate: Haleakala means house-of-the-sun.

The same sun rose over Haleakala's crater for the native, who blessed what he saw, admired the way rain broke light into a rainbow, and made up songs about it. The astronomers do things a different way. To them light is information. It is all they have to tell them about the sun. And because this information comes finely coded, their instruments are designed to fraction it, break it down. The rainbow turns up again on the spectrograph.

Down the beam of light, attenuated by distance, disturbed by atmospheric currents, scattered by interfering particles of floating matter, comes information about the composition, temperature, and behavior of the sun, to be captured on graph paper and film. There are photographs at Haleakala of sunspots, whorls bigger than the earth by multiples, and tongues of million-degree gaseous heat leaping out thousands of miles and licking back. It is all formidable, the source of life laid out for our inspection. So the scientist cuts away fraction by fraction at the incomprehensible.

Astronomers have an institutional need for loneliness. They do not want the companionship of television transmitters, putting out all that electronic noise, or even skiers' huts that would have fires to warm and disturb the atmosphere. To explain the world, they must have the world to themselves.

That is hard to arrange, even for kings of the mountain. At Haleakala, another phenomenon appears on film, weaving an erratic path across the face of the sun. It can be seen with the eye through the objective of the coronagraph, huge, luminescent, transitory. This, it turns out, is not a contribution to science, but a bug. The nesius bug lives at the foot of Haleakala, and flies around modestly there. On warm, still days, the convection currents catch him and waft him up 10,000 feet until he is flying in great numbers over Haleakala, and there he is recorded for science. Among the things we know for certain about life is that the nesius bug, as to light, is highly polarized.

At the foot of Haleakala is Makena beach, a good place for pondering what goes on between the back and the front of the mind. There is good bodysurfing, good fishing, an absence of people. A few hippies live there. They have given up society and most of their clothes. They do their yoga by the water, and learn the best places for coconuts and bananas and avocados. They are not commonsense people. Occasionally they are arrested for trespassing or swimming with nothing on, and then there are court cases about private property and the high tide mark. The magistrate who concerns himself with bare flesh is Japanese. Without any doubt there were communal bathers in his family a generation or two back.

Someone on the beach has certainly been thinking with the front of the brain: trampled into the sand, in figures six feet high, is the complete working out of Maxwell's equation, fundamental in the mathematics of electricity. It is correctly done, but is being washed away by the tide. The same tide has thrown another of those enormous redwood logs on the sand, and its barnacles have one day to evolve. They fail.

Makena will let you know that you have a back to your mind as well as a front, and may even help you to put the two together. And this is always the problem: to put things together. As Gregory Bateson observes, it is not a new problem: we have been taken apart a long time now. But the relation of the part to the whole is everything, and this we have neglected. We have gone through the world cutting narrow, determined paths of progress, making lines from past to present, extending them confidently into the future. We are always arranging things in a commonsense way at one point along the line, only to discover farther along that we may have been plotting collision courses.

So it may be time to stop thinking in terms of lines cut through experience, and time to start thinking in terms of circuits and systems, realizing that an impulse fed into the circuit is bound to run its course, and that a disturbance in one part of the system will surely create disturbances elsewhere.

None of this will be easy. We are not yet good at perceiving systems. We restore an ancient Hawaiian place of refuge on the Big Island, the good idea being to give the modern landscape – which is mostly front – a back once more. So that the restored place will have a look of ancient authenticity, all the introduced plants are sprayed with herbicide and replaced with native species. Then the herbicides wash down into the water and disturb the ancient ecology of the shallows, turning the sea an un-Hawaiian modern green.

This will happen again and again. Still we must go on trying to make the right connections, to reconcile the front of the mind with the back, firm land with shifting sea, the common sense with the richly ambiguous, the prose of life with the poetry, the reasons of reason with the reasons of the heart. If we can complete the circle, heal ourselves, make ourselves whole, we will have found our proper direction.

Above: Young clamdigger, Kaneohe Bay, windward Oahu.
Right: Clam season opening day, Kaneohe Bay.

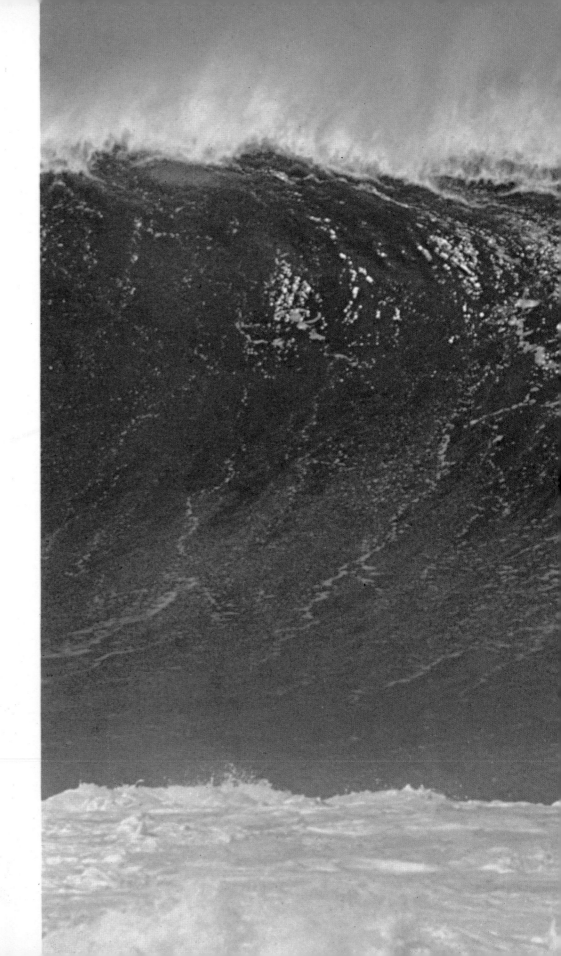

Surfer and wave, Waimea Bay, windward Oahu.

VIII Celebrations

I asked Kawena Pukui, at the end of a long day: what is the nicest thing that ever happened to you?

"What a question!" she said. "There have been so many nice things I can't remember them all."

There is this to celebrate in Hawaii – that ordinary people, by and large, have been able to make a good life for themselves. Somehow, in this small, cramped place, we have managed to avoid pressing each other to the limit. We have found ways to grow to our own shape, freedom to be ourselves.

Perhaps this is the end product of abstractions. Everyone here will tell you in great and circumstantial detail about the accommodating nature of the Hawaiian, the polite reserve of the Oriental who does not push himself forward, the genuine philanthropic sense and goodheartedness of the best of the Puritan haoles, in and out of power. All these formulations are cliches now, but they have become cliches precisely because their essential truth has been demonstrated so often. If we tend to think still in stereotypes, at least we are not unpleasant or vicious about it: we have not blocked our horizons with looming figures of imagined hostility.

Perhaps, on the other hand, our good fortune emerges from something more easily measurable. Perhaps it is just that we are all minorities here. We cannot now imagine any other way.

In any case, our differences are what we live by. They are what we offer each other, and they are offered and accepted as gifts. And so, having gone our own peculiar idiosyncratic way and turned out well enough to please ourselves, we can go on to a belief in the goodness of life. This makes for a sweetness of spirit.

In the strict world view, we might very well be described as amiable but self-deluded. It is easy to point out that times have not always been good here, and may well be bad again – especially if too much of the world's brute reason forces its way in upon us.

Still, the sweetness is here, unmistakably: people respond to it, and with good luck we will have the pleasure of its company a while longer.

I had stayed with the old man on the beach for several days and he had been kind to me. Before leaving, I gave him a carton of cigarettes and a bottle of wine in thanks for his hospitality and fishing advice. And I also left some line, hooks and sinkers.

I was saying goodbye and he shyly handed me a cowrie shell. The shiny, speckled and half-eggshaped object was the traditional Hawaiian octopus lure. Two holes were drilled in it and a hook barb stuck out of one end. In olden days the hook was made of bone or shell but this one was of thick brass rod, laboriously bent and patiently hand-filed and sharpened.

The lure represented much work on the part of the old man. It had not been done idly and he was proud of it. I thanked him. Certainly, it had no value to me other than a souvenir. But it would have been an insult to refuse it. To him, it was a utensil of value. The best way he could show me friendship was to give me something of himself and that was what he had done.

I was touched by the gift. And the more I think of it, the less it becomes an object on my shelf.

Improvers, commonsense men, used to lament that it was hard to get anything done here, that Hawaii was twenty years behind the times. Now it turns out that to be ahead of the times, the urban times at least, is not an unmixed blessing. Things can be done at great speed here these days – anything you want – and if we have not closed that twenty-year gap it might just be because some of us are not altogether sure we want to go precisely where others have led. We might better go on being ourselves. In the meantime we have a period of grace.

To be graced with good fortune is to have avoided bad. In this the islands have been superbly lucky (at least since the black days of disease among the natives, and over that no one had any control at all). Karl Marx wrote somewhere that history occurs twice, first as tragedy, then as farce. Marx was never in Hawaii. We order things differently here, and celebrate the fact.

The islands have had next to nothing to do with the conventional tragic European version of history. We have not gone in for remorselessness and the holding of long grudges. No senseless wars of religion or ideology have been fought on this soil. No man in Hawaii died at the hands of the state for his ideas. The revolution of 1893 that brought down the kingdom ended in less than a week and cost no lives. The royalist counter-revolution of 1895 failed on the same scale; someone summed it up as one man dead and three days without a shave. It was not tried again – no farce, no twice-told tale.

The real and recent revolution, the emancipation of the working man and the appearance of an Oriental middle class, was a revolution of rising expectations, generally gratified. The industrial revolution came in secondhand, in dribs and drabs: no grimed, toiling cities. Death accompanied it only rarely, as such things go.

Tragedy – brief agony – did come in at Pearl Harbor, and young men had to go to war again in Korea and Vietnam. The National Memorial Cemetery of the Pacific is in Punchbowl crater above the city of Honolulu, and the flowers are always fresh there, on the graves of ordinary men. Conventional modern heroes of the sort who climb eagerly to a statue over piles of bodies – these we do not have. That too is worth celebrating.

Not long after the war, when it was proposed that the army of the dead in Punchbowl be ranked with crosses on the graves, Dan Inouye, a Christian, spoke against the idea. There are Buddhists, Jews, and non-believers in Punchbowl, equally to be honored. Punchbowl now has flat markers in a sweep of green grass. There are many ways to God. Celebrate that.

At a fishing place on Oahu, out on a point where lava-bluffs drop sharply into the sea, there is a small shrine. It is merely a rough concrete pillar, inscribed with a few Japanese characters, near where a pole-fisherman stumbled to death in rock-roiled surf. The marker was erected in his memory years ago.

Until recently, this was a treeless, desolate place, one reason I liked it, perhaps. But now, large and expensive homes are being built along the brief cliffs. A haole man from the mainland bought the land a short time back and didn't know what the spire was. He planned to knock it down in landscaping.

Then, on a day before construction started, he saw a tiny, dark-frocked Japanese woman tenderly placing flowers at the base of the marker. He is a good man and understood.

Now, it is enclosed by a neat little fence on manicured grounds of his fine home. And the widow and her grown children have his invitation to visit any time they wish.

By official designation, Hawaii does have two heroes. As a State of the Union, we are entitled to two pedestals for exhibiting our notables at Statuary Hall in Washing-

Below: Golfer waiting to tee off, windward Oahu.
Right: Cheering section, highschool football game, Honolulu, Oahu.

Left: Highschool football player, Honolulu, Oahu.
Below: Miss International Surf, Makaha surfing contest, Oahu.
Right: Highschool basketball player, Honolulu, Oahu.

Above: Children at annual Filipino
Santa Cruzan Festival, Honolulu, Oahu.
Opposite: Filipina-American woman portraying
Queen Helena of Greece in Santa Cruzan
procession, Honolulu.

Above: Marker for unidentified Pearl Harbor dead, Memorial Day, Punchbowl Crater, National Memorial Cemetery of the Pacific, Honolulu, Oahu.

Right: Family portrait at graveside, Memorial Day, Punchbowl, Honolulu.

ton. The first choice was inescapable – Kamehameha, defined as The Great, the unifier, benign despot. Westerners are amazed at him, and can respond to him. The second candidate for official greatness took more thinking about. The decision fell again on a man who had something to do with death, but in a compassionate way – the Belgian priest Damien of Molokai. He chose life with the lepers, suffered disease, disfigurement and death, and will very likely be a saint one day.

He and Kamehameha in replica stop traffic at Statuary Hall, the superbly intelligent civilized savage in gilt, and the likely saint in bronze, among all those solid marble republicans. In Honolulu, not far from the Kamehameha statue on King Street, the original statue of Damien by Marisol Escobar stands in the forecourt of the new state capitol. Mercifully, the artist does not have him succoring a stricken child. There he is, all alone, blocky, stocky, unlovely, leper-faced, falling-eared, with his wire rimmed glasses under his homely hat, his shrivelled carpenter's hands once apt for coffin-making, his peasant boots sticking out under his priest's habit. A great and humble man, with his own toughness and satisfaction in the beauty of his fearful vocation; a fine and sanguine work of art, with its own reverence.

The Hawaiians themselves do well by the celebrations at statues, especially for a people diminished by civilization and its introduced diseases. They do not, they say, mourn the death of the great men; they celebrate their lives, and by extension life itself. A warming distinction, and one which we all manage to observe.

By and large – to repeat – we are remarkably free of the oppressions of the past, to the point where we feel free to play with history, use it for our amusement.

Whether this shows proper respect for the back of the mind is debatable. But our private lives show more sensitivity and grace than some of our public celebrations.

Take the Aloha Week parade. It was invented to fill up a valley in the graphs of hotel occupancy in October. It has grown into some of everything. The politicians waving silver-haired from limousines, a prance of pretty girls on horseback representing the various islands, Marine bands, the resurrected Royal Hawaiian Guard with white helmets, muttonchop whiskers and mustaches, marching societies, floats, floats, floats, baton-twirlers, the older Hawaiians wilting a little in the heat – they all trek from Ala Moana through Waikiki, attended by clowns and Chinese Shriners on motorscooters. People enjoy it. But what is it telling us? Perhaps that, being a democracy, we get the processions we deserve.

We work hard to show the tourist how we can celebrate. In the end, though, it is likely that the tourist does not come to Hawaii for celebrations of a public kind. He is about his own observances. He is looking to liberate himself from what he is. That arranges itself. The elemental iconography of warm islands is gently subversive of cold continental civilization: the amniotic easefulness of the warm salt water within the reef, the genital candor of the coconut palm, the outright sexual impudence of the anthurium. The tourist celebrates release. He unstraps his wristwatch, puts on loud shorts and a straw hat with a plastic palm tree growing out the top, and exposes his knees to sunburn. This is his way of signalling he knows civilization is inhibition and work without joy a waste of life. And with any luck this will give him a more balanced attitude to the labor he must take up again when he goes home.

KAMEHAMEHA

Below: Hawaiian portraying alii,
Aloha Week Parade, Honolulu.
Right: Samoan woman, Samoan Flag Day
celebrations, Ala Moana Park, Honolulu, Oahu.

Below left: Pau rider, Kamehameha Day
Parade, Honolulu, Oahu.

Below right: Hawaiian portraying alii,
Ulu Mau Village, windward Oahu.

Opposite: Aloha Week torchlight procession,
Waikiki Beach.

Overleaf left: Shriner as clown,
Aloha Week Parade, Honolulu.

Overleaf right: Hawaiian offering sweet potato,
City of Refuge dedication, Island of Hawaii.

Preceding spread: Hula dancer, Aloha Week Parade,
Honolulu, Oahu.

Below: Samoans at Flag Day celebrations,
Ala Moana Park, Honolulu.

Right: Samoan children in traditional dance,
Flag Day celebrations, Honolulu.

After fifteen years I went back to Massachusetts and my mother told me I'd been in love with Hawaii ever since I was a tiny boy. When I got my first geography book I showed her pictures of Hawaii in it and said I would go there someday.

She told me this one night in the old house near Boston with the New England winter outside, the promise of snow in air and elms stark and leafless under highway lights. There was a vase of pussywillows on the table and my father smoked his pipe and watched me. He was silent, tired, and for the first time I noticed he was old.

"You read everything you could about Hawaii," she said. "Don't you remember?"

I'd had no conscious thought of it for years. Memories-imagined and memories-real tend to erase each other. But I remembered now.

We drank tea and my father saucered his for cooling as he always had. The kitchen smells were the same, fresh bread, Granger tobacco and residual aromas of supper. There was frost on the window and I was to leave the next day. It had been fifteen years since they'd seen me. One brother had been killed in the war and the other had left to go his way; my sister was soon to be married and they would be alone.

I knew what was coming and my mother said it sadly, as close to pleading as she allowed herself.

"Do you have to go back?"

I answered yes—such a simple word—and stumbled explanations about work and promises.

But my mind was on that lacing of frost on the windowsill and wind moaning in naked trees and I knew island wind-songs and gentleness were not far away. And I knew Hawaii always had been my spirit home, always would be, and it could not be explained to these sad and loved old faces, waiting out their days in harshness.

If the tourist business is full of people with Hawaiian blood, it is because they know best how to help the tourist in his celebrations, just as they have always helped people here in the same way. Hawaiians have the finest of celebratory senses. They are natural guests, natural hosts, blessers of enterprise, general gracers of occasion. The kahuna for hire – and he is something of a fashion – will christen a newly finished house with pourings of gin and brandy, and he will really be using word magic. Kini for gin and palani for brandy are words going back to the first toasts drunk between Hawaiians and Westerners. Longer ago kini meant multitudinous, as in blessings, and palani meant to touch the heavens.

Because the Hawaiians are best at celebrating, other people, and especially haoles, have picked up some of their language and use it as word magic to brighten life. Listen, and you will hear haoles using Hawaiian words for affection, fecundity, welcome, feasting.

The luau is a formal feast of great jollity. It has been taken over by the most solemn haoles. The golden wedding anniversary of a haole couple whose families go back to missionary times will likely be celebrated Hawaiian-style, and there will surely be singing of the sweet old Hawaiian songs and some dancing of the hula. Inside every well-fleshed Hawaiian is a slender hula dancer waiting to be let out. The grace is likely to issue through the fingertips. It is the same with the staid haole. He co-opts the Hawaiian sense of occasion, and finds, rather to his surprise, that he can dance. Not the staid businessman's bounce of sociable duty, but a dance all his own, in which the body and the language of gesture count at their full worth in the celebration of life.

Just lately a new race of dancing celebrants has

appeared in the islands, young haoles mostly, washed up from the floating world of the mainland, though they have been joined by some local boys and girls. They are the hippies, tribespeople living on the fringes of the larger tribes of society. Whether they celebrate as others do, out of a wish to make some poetic connections between past and future, it is hard to tell. Certainly they have rummaged time and place, and live for the moment in pleasant confusion. They eat less than most other sorts of people, share more, and seem to like what they are doing. They seem to be floating, but perhaps it is only on meditation. In any case their mild disorientation suits them, and they smile a lot, gently, out of their private immersion in the cosmos.

They have taken to gathering at New Year, great nebulae of them, in the crater of Diamond Head, a serene and silent and beautiful place above Waikiki. They help the sun come up with chanting and drumming, and pass the rest of the day in a state of being, singing, dancing, painting their bodies, nursing their children.

They think of themselves as witnessing the dawn of the age of Aquarius, or the beginning of the end of the world. In the crater a boy of eighteen quietly arranges piles of grass cuttings into a peace symbol, and sits for hours in the middle of his magic circle, in the full lotus position of a Buddhist adept, with his version of grace issuing through his fingertips, his hands moving from one mudra to another, in the way of the great Buddha himself, meditating, witnessing, teaching.

So we go, grave and gay – dancers, all of us, to the music of time, rehearsing the movements that others have taught us, or that we have half forgotten and must rescue from forgetfulness. We stir, reach, pause, hesi-tate, waiting for the sacred order of things to leap into a single magnificent shape before us, lifting us above the forced march of daily life, allowing us a perception of eternity, the circle of sacred timelessness.

So many of us leave now, from time to time, to view wonders of far places, conduct commerce in smogged cities, walk the memory-haunted streets of youth.

And we come home, hanai children of the mother-islands.

Perhaps part of the reason lies in our adoption – I have never been able to explain it – but there is an overwhelming singularity in coming home here.

We come back now in great aircraft that float down to burst through cloud floors and hang suspended for a moment over the beauty – the infinite sea, the sun path in its billion-footed dance on water, the mountain islands dark and soft.

Like guardians of a familiar walkway, Molokai lazes on one side, with battered cliffs and beach lacings, Oahu on the other, the fluted crags of the Koolaus scattering tiny islets offshore. Maui is in the distance and if the day is right, Mauna Kea looms far away.

The good, great islands, afloat on the deepest and bluest of oceans, announcing all the warmth and beauties to be found later in their embrace.

So often, in returning, I remember the answer of a new friend, long evenings ago, when I asked him where he had been born.

"Here in Hawaii," he said, "when I arrived ten years ago."

This is what our celebrations are about. Some observances are private, but not really: we may take part by respecting privacy, and everyone will be nourished. The Hawaiian Mission Children's Society meets once a year

Above and right: Sunshine Festival celebrants,
inside Diamond Head Crater, Oahu.

274

Above left and right: Island musicians,
rock concert, windward Oahu.

Opposite: Sunshine Festival dancer,
Diamond Head Crater, Honolulu.

Above: Island girl at Art Park Festival,
Honolulu, Oahu.

Right: Japanese Noh drama character,
Punahou School, Honolulu.

to count heads. As each reverberating pioneer name is called, the descendants of the old families stand. There is proud competition in numbers. When the Judds do not win, the Cookes do, with fifty or sixty members present, or more. The oldest member is always over eighty; there is always a youngest member, a baby, to be held. On the Society's genealogical charts, which reach back to colonial New England, there have been Hawaiian names linked with the haole for two or three generations now, and lately an Oriental name or two. These are islands of the gentlest invasions. And somehow the closer we live to each other, the more space we all seem to have, the more we are enlarged. Celebrate that.

"You love it here, don't you?" the question comes. "Why?"

How is it answered? Do I love it here after all these years? Or has it been an accident of existence, an escape, an ennui of acceptance? Years piling one on top of the other in a soft place until now there are so many? Like an old marriage, unquestioned, warm and secure. So I close my eyes and try to think the answer. A true one.

Place the words one on top of another, and it comes up that I am not absolutely sure. Aren't all loves – peoples, places – prisons of a sort?

I came here young and hungry, away from harshness, sameness, poorness – running from youth. I saw a poster on the wall of the postoffice in Boston during a terrible winter and it changed my life. It said that sheetmetalworker's helpers were needed at a place called Pearl Harbor, Territory of Hawaii and that was enough. And my father and his friends were willing to lie a little bit and sign papers that I was qualified. I came and it was the great adventure: catapulted in a fine train over great states – only colored jigsaw pieces of map before – roaring over the West, the linen and heavy silver of the dining car . . .

And one early morning, on the Texas Panhandle, a cowboy riding against the sky as if to say, I have been placed here to gallop in lovely silhouette beside this train, as a sample of sights and wonders to come . . .

And then we crossed the ocean and I met the others, from all over the country and we arrived at dawn. It was love all right then, with islands and sky becoming one, taking shape out of night, and the scent of flowers and woodsmoke off the land.

I am not one to remember dates and days clearly, but I remember being young and the sea and sky vivid and the marvel of the beauty; water and air that sparkled and the bleakness behind me. When I'm old I will remember this air, but it will be the air of long ago when I was young; air laden with flower and land smells, the stirring of the islands . . .

I remember the early work, because it was dirty work with hot metal and sparks and grease, and I have always disliked such work. But it was accomplishment too, when the steel was fitted, the job done and the ship went out and I could say I was part of that. There's a sort of love in that too. And there was love of companions and our talk and appetites for living and sharing with one another. We pawned watches and shared the money to eat until the first payday and then spent most of it on beer and laughter.

Those of us who came long ago have gone so many separate ways, and it is all for the good. I entertained twelve Congressmen for a client not long ago – and had breakfast with the Governor, privately, last week. The man with whom I pawned watches is living out in a little house in Nanakuli with a Hawaiian wife and eight kids and still working for the government. He made his choice and I mine and we're both happy for ourselves and still see each other in friendship.

I suppose I have loved it here, still do. Yes. I can say it out and mean it.

Because it has loved me, this place, Hawaii.

High summer in the islands is the time for the Buddhist festival of Bon-odori. Its ceremonies have to do with death, but more with life, the continuity of things, the stages of the immense journey upon which we all travel, the living and the remembered dead.

The Japanese take time to tidy up the family shrines in their homes, and go to the family plot in the cemetery to hang lanterns and leave oranges and rice cakes at the foot of the gravestones. After the sun sets, there will be a night of dancing in the temple yard.

The Bon dance, like everything else in Hawaii, has been through its changes.

At Haleiwa, a tiny town on the north shore of Oahu, there is always a big crowd. High on a lantern-decked platform, the drummers and chanters begin their music. A great circle of dancers forms. They step simply and subtly, in an endless rhythm of advance, retreat, advance again. Everyone dances. The plantation worker goes by, masked, intent, serious, private in public; the housewife, transfigured in kimono and grave powder-white face. A small girl, part-haole, follows her mother step after step, learning. A middle-aged man, here from Japan to visit relatives, dances precisely and securely, far from home, yet at home.

The evening is endless. Dancers drop out, talk with friends, sip a drink, then dance again; the circles form and break and re-form. Some haole women from one of the military posts have been watching. They try a few steps on their own, then a few more, and are dancing, part of the circle. Theirs is a different tradition; they do not get things quite right, but the circle does not exclude them, it catches them up and wheels on just the same – people may dance well or less well here, it is not important. A flourish of teenagers gets impatient. Boys and girls join hands and skip madly in a tight centrifugal circle around the drummers' platform for five minutes, and collapse laughing. Their mothers dance sedately on the circumference; the children have passed them twenty times.

Earlier this night there has been a meteor shower, flashing, evanescent. Now the sky over the shore is open, unbroken by cloud, ceremonial black, brilliant with stars – a time for good seeing. It is the moment for the floating lanterns to go out to sea. The children light candles. The lanterns, hundreds of them, pass one by one from the hands of the priest to barefoot men who set them down in the shallows, and the current gradually takes hold and sweeps the flickering flotilla out to sea in a great curve of light. The spirits of the dead, reassured by remembrance, content with the dance, will depart with the lanterns.

There is a rising swell on the reef. The lanterns tilt and ride. Every so often a wave picks one up and speeds it down to extinction. The rest go on their way, distant now. The candles gutter, but burn still. Separation is felt but never final. There will be a Bon dance next year, and the next, and the next.

This is the ritual of one faith. But it is also, as men of all faiths here can see, a celebration of the mystery of every man's life – – "The frail boat, the light brave but small, the rising and falling of the waters, the enfolding darkness and the watchers on the shore . . . "

Chinese New Year celebration.
Maunakea Street, Honolulu, Oahu.

Right: Lighting incense sticks, Kwan Yin Temple, Honolulu, Oahu.
Far right: Chinese lion dancer, Honolulu.

Right: Okinawan dance, Honolulu, Oahu.
Overleaf: Floating lanterns lighting way
for spirits, O'Bon Festival, Haleiwa, Oahu.

On Camera Equipment and Printing

The cameras and lenses I use in executing projects like THE HAWAIIANS are central to everything I hope to achieve.

My investment is high. Three years or more of my professional life, my reputation in this field, future income from the sale of photographs to clients, all rest on the quality of the cameras and lenses chosen.

For the last ten years I have used only Nikons.

My reason is simply that it is the best system of photography I can imagine. I own, as do many other professionals, a dozen or so camera bodies, thirty-two lenses at last count, from the fish-eye to the 800mm Tele-Nikkor, and motor drives and accessories that I have lost count of. I use them all. And when I need them, they work.

What may interest the non-professional is the fact that most of this book was done with a single Nikkormat FTN and three or four lenses. The Nikon F is superb, but for day in and day out photography, the Nikkormat is my idea of a perfect instrument. And the Nikkormat **works** day in and day out. I regularly produce Ektacolor prints from Nikkormat transparencies that range up to three by five feet in size.

In the darkroom I use DURST enlargers for the same reason I use Nikon in the field. They are precise, fast, extremely well designed and manufactured. Working on layouts, I often will make 400 to 500 prints of varying size in a single day. Without the DA-900, I would never be able to achieve this kind of production.

All mural exhibit color printing for our project has been done by Rapid Color Inc. in Glendale, California. Ten years ago Rapid Color produced for me a large Type C color print that was the finest C print I had ever seen.

Over the years they have maintained their lead in the field and today produce color exhibit prints that, in my opinion, are unequalled in the United States.

In Hawaii, I was fortunate to have available the personal services of Henk Kuiper and his color laboratory, Master Color. Throughout the project, Master Color produced consistently fine internegatives, color duplicates, lay-out prints, and master Ektacolor prints for reproduction. Kuiper's professional help and personal friendship have been invaluable to our efforts.

Robert B. Goodman

Behind the Photographs

Cover. For the first eighteen months of the project that produced this book, one question came at me again and again, "What do you plan to put on the cover?" My answer was that the cover had to be a face, probably a young girl, and that I would know the *right* face the minute I saw it. Later, to find that face, I spent a day checking the hula schools in Honolulu. April Kaiolani Hoopai, part Hawaiian, Japanese, and Caucasian, was in a class for eight year olds when I saw her, and I never had a moment's doubt. A phone call to her mother, a test roll of film shot quickly, and the following Sunday, a full-scale test shooting by the Kahala Hilton hotel. The wind was very strong, the light variable, and the nearest florist shop was overstocked with maiden's hair fern. The 400mm f/4.5 Nikkor lens was on a tripod to steady it, Ektachrome-X film in the Nikon F to provide a rich color effect. One thirtieth of a second wide-open was the limit of the light and what followed was nine rolls of every bit of cajolery I could think of to catch and hold her attention. One frame out of more than 300 test shots made further shooting unnecessary.

Page 6. Sometimes the right picture happens for the wrong reason. The fact is that the woman didn't want to be photographed and decided to hide behind her infant child. Nikkormat FTN, 105mm lens, and Ektachrome-X film.

Pages 12-13. This was to be a big production shot. Phone calls to the Captain of the barquentine, a check with the weatherman to fix the time of sunset, more calls to confirm the availability of the helicopter. Three Nikons were loaded with Kodachrome II, and 28mm, 55mm, and 105mm lenses were tucked in the gadget bag in easy reach. The rest turned out to be very simple: the helicopter climbed up and down, flew this way and that and hovered until I had photographed from every angle I could think of. There is a limit to the magic you can work into any preconceived photograph; this is because preconception almost always limits the possibilities of the moment itself. In this case I knew what I wanted and when I had it on film, I went home.

Pages 14-15. The 200mm and 105mm lenses are ideal for this kind of situation photography, Nikkormat FTN.

Pages 16-17. Simple, direct, declarative photography, and the single lens reflex gives one almost complete control over the final image. The bather was taken with the 400mm tele-Nikkor, the full page picture with the 200mm, and the others with the 105mm lens.

Pages 20-21 (left). I had a friend along in my Cessna Skyhawk for a dawn flight to the Big Island. I saw this picture coming, and the Micro-Nikkor lens plus some very fast film advancing gave me a series of pictures through the plastic windshield of the airplane. In a situation like this there is just no time to think about exposure, and the center-weighted metering took care of it all. Relatively slow shutter speed blurred the propeller, and the star effect is fairly predictable when shooting through plexiglass. Kodachrome II film.

Pages 20-21 (below). The remarkable lack of internal flare in Nikkor optics helped make possible the small picture of the north coast of Molokai. So did the fact that I accidentally had the right lens on (105mm), Kodachrome II

in the Nikkormat, and enough sense to look back over my shoulder to see if the backlighting had made the scene I had just flown by any more exciting.

Pages 22-23 (left). It was a rain shower in the channel that separates the big island of Hawaii from the islands of Maui and Kahoolawe. Back lighting makes the event more visible, and Ektachrome-X film and a 28mm lens on the FTN did the rest. Exposure needle was centered.

Pages 22-23 (below). In the smaller picture, a low light level made it necessary to put on a 35mm f/2 lens so that a 250th of a second shutter speed could be used. Ektachrome-X and the Nikkormat.

Pages 24-25 (left). Midway Island is part of the Hawaiian Chain that runs all the way to Kure or Ocean Island. Midway, if you are lucky enough to get there, is a bird-watcher's paradise. In certain areas the ground is covered with nesting sooty terns. This picture could have been taken by anyone with any camera. I used a Nikon F, 35mm lens and Kodachrome.

Pages 24-25 (below). The smaller picture took more effort. The fairy terns were high in an ironwood tree and I used the 300mm Nikkor lens on a Nikon F. Exposure and sun position was varied extensively and this frame is only one of many different usable photographs that resulted. Kodachrome II film.

Pages 28-29 (right). The feeling of new life unfolding was overwhelming in this frond of a tree fern. I was hiking with my wife and children and some friends high in the mountains overlooking Honolulu. The Micro-Nikkor lens and Ektachrome-X for the grey day, and a tripod-less grab-shot gave me the picture. But if I had it to do over again, I would absolutely use a tripod.

Pages 28-29 (far right). The silversword plant *was* taken with the Nikkormat on a tripod. A 24mm lens and a cold wet miserable grey morning on the clinkered rim of Haleakala Crater on the Island of Hawaii were two of the ingredients. My wife, Barbara, was scouting out photogenic plants. There was only one frame of the Ektachrome-X film, out of several hundred that, for me, caught the magic of the place.

Pages 30-31 (right). The only thing that sets this picture apart is the water reflecting the evening sky. Reflections are always useful to temporarily puzzle the viewer so that he will look again. As part of this *take,* I moved in with a telephoto and built images out of the intertwining of the palm trunks. But these turned out to be mostly design exercises with very little emotional content. It is a constant problem — for me at least — to decide which way to go between design and emotion, so I generally shoot from both directions, hoping to close in on one image with both design qualities and emotional content. 105mm lens, Nikkormat FTN, Kodachrome II, camera resting on the open door of our automobile — with the motor stopped to avoid vibrations.

Pages 34-35 (below). Easy photographs first. The god figure was taken shortly after sunrise with a 28mm lens, Nikkormat FTN and the sun barely visible behind the head of the carved image. Broadly bracketed in exposure for a variety of effects. Kodachrome II.

Pages 34-35 (right). How do you expose for the moon's bright surface and for the dark sky both? How to get separation behind the island and for the moon path all in one frame — and in color yet? First get a very accurate spot meter to read the moon's face. Then set your camera on a tripod firmly planted in the beach sand. Marking your film properly, shoot 36 exposures of the island and the moon path, then back up the film to its original mark and, changing lenses, shoot 36 exposures again with the image of the moon about where you want it. If you bracket exposures a bit on both trips thru the camera, chances are you'll have a remarkable image. Trickery? Rather than argue the question, I prefer to use as my guideline, the effect the image has on the viewer.

Pages 38-39 (left). The volcano was erupting near the bottom of the Halemaumau Firepit on the Big Island of Hawaii. It was a clear night over the volcano area with a light wind blowing. After the first few nights of photographing a volcano, new ideas for exciting photographs come less frequently. So more out of curiosity than anything else I set up the tripod, focused the 50mm f/2 lens on infinity and started a wide bracket running from 30 seconds all the way down to 1 second. This picture resulted and I'm happy I made the effort. Kodachrome is the only 35mm color film I know of that will so regularly tolerate excessively long exposures.

Pages 40-41 (left and right). To get a picture like this (a wide angle shot that is every bit as close to the flying lava as it looks) ideally you have to be very brave and a bit stupid. With those two qualifications practically any camera will do if you go this close to an erupting volcano. I happened to use the Nikon F and the 28mm lens with Kodachrome. The same combination was used for the smaller picture but with camera tripod-mounted and exposures widely bracketed at dawn.

Pages 42-43 (right). It took me better than an hour to climb my Cessna Skyhawk to the 15,750 feet from which this picture was taken, and I was fortunate that it was one of those infrequent days when the upper winds were nonexistent. I circled the summit slowly again and again, my oxygen mask constantly getting in the way of my camera. My window was open and on each pass of the cratered summit I would get three or four frames with the FTN and its 28mm lens. Kodachrome II and a Nikon polarizing filter were the tools that added visual drama to the scene. Exposure was by the needle but above and below as well for good measure.

Pages 46-47 (left). I've always gotten pleasure out of taking a 24mm or 28mm lens on a Nikon, putting the camera solidly on a tripod, stopping the lens all the way down and then with the extreme depth of field available, making a picture. This was one of those moments and Kodachrome II delivered the color quality and resolution. It was a 28mm lens this time.

Pages 50-51 (left). The phallic rock on the Island of Molokai posed few photographic problems. It was located in a clearing, the light strong and diffuse. The problem was catching the line and massive maleness of it. I used a 35mm lens, the FTN, and a tripod. Ektachrome-X.

Pages 50-51 (above). There was far more of a problem in photographing the ''birthing stones'', a collection of strangely shaped rocks in a clearing in a pineapple field in Central Oahu. I made four trips to the location before I found the right light — a long slanting evening sun to accentuate the undulating porosity of the stones. The hole in this rock is thought to be a burial place for the umbilical cord from a newborn child.

Pages 52-53 (left). It gets very hot and dry and uncomfortable spending a day in the middle of a huge lava flow. Even surrounded by the culturally fascinating rock carvings called petroglyphs, enthusiasm eventually wears thin. It is more depressing yet, having photographed all day, to know that the picture you want still is not on your film. It is at this point of mind-numbing fatigue that I stop *thinking* about the picture I want and simply *take* it. Late afternoon sun, the lens hand-shielded, the 20mm Nikkor lens on the FTN. Kodachrome II.

Pages 56-57 (right). For some pictures, being in the right place at the right time is indispensable. This wave picture is a case in point. I spent days trying to get just this photograph and in the end, swallowed my pride and called Honolulu photographer Bob Young, a virtuoso with his Nikons. Bob had taken the picture the year before at Waimea Bay on Oahu, one of the best places for shorebreaks in the islands. Of its kind it's a masterpiece and Bob, for agreeing to its use in this book, has my gratitude as well as my admiration as a fine photographer.

Pages 60-61 (left and below). The big picture is of backlit taro plants from almost ground level. Kodachrome film and a 24mm lens. A planting of new taro becomes a delicate pattern by simply stepping back and using the 200mm lens. Kodachrome II.

Pages 64-65 (right). First you find a friend that has a Questar with a Nikon adaptor. Then you take an old kneesock, to drape over the lens, and fill it full of sand. Third, buy or borrow the biggest tripod you can find and take it to Waikiki Beach about an hour before sunset. And then, rock steady and focused where you think the sun will be, you sit and watch it disappear behind a cloud bank you didn't see, a good twenty minutes before the sun was due to touch the horizon. If you are lucky, the sun makes it all the way to the horizon unobscured, and you get a picture like this. Kodachrome II, Nikon F.

Pages 68-69 (below). The small picture of the fish god is unexceptional. The setting for the picture was something else again. A deserted Hawaiian fishing village on a little-seen corner of Lanai, once the summer home and favorite fishing grounds of Kamehameha the Great.

Pages 68-69 (right). The picture of the frigate bird represents a rare problem in photography and if you are really curious as to how this picture came about, write me care of the publisher and I'll be happy to tell you.

Page 71. Near Keahole, on the big island of Hawaii, are many old Hawaiian paths over the rough lava. This one is marked by the bleached shells of large opihis. On a moonlit nite, the markings would be easy to follow. To heighten the effect of the trail vanishing in the distance, I used a 24mm lens on a Nikkormat FTN, tripod-mounted. Late afternoon sun and Kodachrome II. Lens was hand shielded.

Pages 72-73 (right). Earlier I talked about using tree trunks as design elements in a photograph. Here, at first light, I used the trunks of the palm trees as a varying middleground through which to shoot the carved figures. Look at the picture from the viewpoint of simply seeing the light areas of sky trapped and held by the dark lines of the trees and figures. A 200mm lens, Nikkormat FTN and Kodachrome II, all tripod-mounted.

Pages 74-75 (right). The great god of war, Kukailimoku, who had witnessed all of Kamehameha the Great's victories, is one of the treasures of Honolulu's Bishop Museum, and I am indebted to Museum director Dr.

Roland Force for helping so generously in the making of this picture. It took better than four hours to light and position the image. Two 3200K floods were positioned to reflect brightly off the pearlshell eyes. By exposing for the surface of those eyes, the rest of the image with its featherwork and dog-toothed mouth went dark. Kodachrome Type A film and the Micro-Nikkor lens on a Nikkormat FTN tripod-mounted.

Pages 78-79. Sylvania makes an expensive, but rugged and invaluable, portable floodlight that is indispensable for photographing in burial caves and other remote dark places. With a tripod-mounted Nikkormat FTN, the 24mm lens, Ektachrome Type B, and two Sun Guns, the picture of the petroglyph images of men going off to war was easy prey.

Pages 80-81 (below and right). The small picture on the left is a grab shot that should have been better. The magic word is *tripod* and I simply didn't use one. Nikkormat FT, 105mm lens, Ektachrome-X. The burial cave was in about as inaccessible a spot as I ever care to go. A tortuous jeep ride down a steep Big Island hillside . . . followed by a cramped and angled entrance into a pitch black cave tunnel that went on forever. Inside it was hot, dusty and oppressive. In one area there were skulls everywhere and I used the extremely rugged Sun Guns to make the picture. Rather than overpower the picture with direct light I put in the 350-watt bulbs and bounced the light off the cave ceiling. The tripod-mounted Nikkormat FTN with 20mm lens in place and Ektachrome Type B returned me the picture.

Pages 84-85. I think this is the best picture in the book, but then maybe that's because I remember just how uncomfortable I was taking it. A helicopter had deposited me with my equipment at the water's edge in an isolated area on the Kona Coast of the Big Island. I had come to photograph a large handshaped lava basin, used by the early Hawaiians in obtaining salt from evaporated sea-water. With any luck, I anticipated I would need a half-hour to get the photograph. So I arranged for the helicopter to pick me up then and fly me back to our campsite for the night.
On the Kona Coast, rain was just not on my mind and I puttered around setting up the camera and tripod oblivious to the darkness clouding the air only a few miles south of where I stood. Out to sea the sun was setting. I had filled the lava basin with sea water and was shooting pictures when the first large raindrop hit. Not even looking up, I kept my eye glued to the Nikkormat shooting through a full 36 exposures and shielding the camera with my body, reloading and shooting another roll. Then, looking up, I knew it would be a long wait. A thunderstorm, unusual for the area, had formed above me and I had to race to get my equipment into the Halliburton. An hour later, standing in the heavy rain with lightning and thunder hitting from every quarter, I was beginning to suspect that the Hawaiian gods knew my whereabouts. For all its discomfort, it was a strangely beautiful experience.

Pages 88-89 (right). I had often watched the torch fisherman in the shallow water around the islands. Some used gas mantle lights, others electric torches. Now and again one would appear with a torch made in the old way, a length of bamboo, filled inside with kerosene and with burlap jammed into the top. The burlap acted as a candle wick and if the flame burned low, the fisherman had only to turn the torch upside down and shake to renew the flame.

We started long before dawn, and, in the absolute darkness of night, there was no possible way to separate the sky, or horizon or water from the figure of the man. Kodachrome II was mandatory for the lengthy exposures used. The Nikkormat FTN was tripod-mounted and waist-deep in the water with me. The first light of a dawn sky made all the difference, and a few long exposures later the fisherman and I were headed back to shore, each of us with our catch for the night's work.

Pages 90-91 (left). First light on the southeastern coast of Maui, high speed Ektachrome, the 35mm f/2 Nikkor on a Nikkormat FTN, and a handheld exposure. The film recorded the extreme blueness of first light shadows and the picture of the net fisherman was used as color counterpoint to the large image to its right.

Pages 90-91 (right). The 105mm lens, a highly diffused morning sun and the shallow water of the southern coast of Molokai all become part of this image of two isolated fishermen surrounded by an expanse of monochromatic sea and sky. Nikkormat FTN, Kodachrome II.

Pages 92-93 (left). The 200mm Nikkor is ideal for flattening perspective just enough to establish a two-dimensional pattern for a photograph. This Hawaiian farmer planting taro offers a case in point. Nikkormat FTN, Ektachrome-X.

Pages 92-93 (right). 55mm Micro-Nikkor, Nikkormat FTN, Ektachrome-X.

Pages 96-97 (right). The drive along the northwestern tip of the big island is one of the most beautiful drives in the world. Soft, rolling grass-covered hillsides slope seaward to be backlit by the evening sun. The lens was screened by the needles of an ironwood tree. I watched the horse watch me. The sun flooding into the 200mm lens helped create the mood of the photograph as did the horse's fortuitous tail flick and the bending of his foreleg. The Nikkormat allows you the luxury of knowing where every element of the picture will be. Note the dead tree in the photograph's upper left. Kodachrome II.

Pages 100-101 (left). Not far from where the horse was photographed I went searching for a tombstone Honolulu photographer David Cornwell had shown once in a movie. Walking through a silent jungle of giant bamboo I came upon the giant banyan tree and the cross it had enveloped. The 24mm lens, tripod-mounted Nikkormat FTN, and Ektachrome-X made the photograph with ease.

Pages 100-101 (right). The church is severe in architectural purity and it was this simplicity of form and line that was important to me. Kodachrome II, a 20mm Nikkor lens, and the Nikkormat FTN were used.

Pages 102-103 (above). She was in the gallery of the House during the traditional flower-packed opening of the State Legislature. The tripod-mounted 400mm Nikkor was just right for the job. The camera was the Nikkormat FTN, the film High Speed Ektachrome Type-B.

Pages 102-103 (right). Kawaiahao Church, is one of Hawaii's great historic buildings. Its coral block construction needed a certain sunlight to accentuate the texture of the building's surface. Moving behind a giant plant, its silhouette framing the church, gives the picture drama. 20mm Nikkor lens, Kodachrome II, and the Nikkormat FTN.

Pages 108-109 (above and right). Both of these pictures were taken within a very short

time. The young fisherman with his spear and lobsters was caught against a setting sun by the 200mm Nikkor. The youths listening to the young Maui fisherman with upraised arm were grouped in late sunlight that was just too mood-provoking for me to resist raising my camera. The 24mm wide angle lens solved the viewpoint problem and the Nikkormat FTN metering system took care of exposure.

Pages 110-111 (right). It was toward the end of the luau, a birthday party at their Makena home for a Hawaiian couple named Johnny and Angie Luuai. There had been luau pig, poi and yams, crunchy black crab and lomi lomi salmon, opihi and a huge bowl of raw tuna and seaweed. Tens of dozens of bottles of local Primo beer cooled the mid-day for the guests with myriad bottles still in reserve in ice-filled washtubs. In the softness of late afternoon the guitars were brought out and the singing began. There was gentleness, and a delight in the words and melody. It was the sweetness of sound that comes from the Hawaiian at home. I photographed to the rhythm and warmth of the moment, felt embarrassed by the mechanical intrusion of my camera, laid it aside finally and joined in the singing.

Pages 114-115 (right and left). The funeral of Duke Kahanamoku, the Hawaiian athlete who won greatness for himself in Olympic competition, was a phenomenon equal to the life of the man it intended to honor. It was a "beachboy funeral," half-Hollywood and half-Hawaiian, with the ashes borne out to sea by a fleet of outrigger canoes. Less than a mile offshore they were committed to the waters with leis and wreaths of maile vine. The paddlers then raced their outriggers back to shore and the huge crowds that had darkened the beach under a grey and rainfilled sky began to disperse, knowing that something of importance, somehow, had passed them by. The youth of today talk of "vibrations" and the edge of the sea was full of them this day. Even now, this far removed from the moment, it is difficult for me to put my feelings that day into words. Two Nikkormats, 105mm and 200mm lenses and Ektachrome-X film.

Pages 118-119 (below). Aerial, 105mm lens, Nikkormat FTN, Kodachrome II.

Pages 118-119 (right). The problem was a dramatic shot of sugar cane. Sunrise, the Nikkormat FTN on a tripod, 105 lens, Kodachrome II. Exposure was bracketed so that final choice could be made on the editing table.

Pages 120-121 (left). Both pictures, 105mm lens, Kodachrome II, Nikkormat FTN.

Pages 120-121 (right). Again, the 105mm lens, Ektachrome-X and the Nikkormat.

Pages 124-125 (below and right). All pictures with the 55mm Micro-Nikkor lens, Kodachrome II film, and all pictures taken with the Nikkormat on a tripod.

Pages 128-129 (left). The older Japanese-Americans were gathered in Honolulu for a ceremony in their honor. The lighting was abysmal — too flat and mixed with some mercury vapor light. But the 400mm Tele-Nikkor on a tripod got the images on Type-B Ektachrome with razor sharpness and superb contrast in the most difficult area of all, the shadows. The camera's internal metering gave me two days of errorless exposures.

Pages 128-129 (right). Handheld Nikkormat FTN 28mm, Kodachrome II.

Pages 132-133. There were two possible ways to achieve this photograph. One would make use of Nikon's panoramic tripod attachment. The other, and the one I elected, was to use

my 35mm Panon Widelux camera. For all the sweep of this spread, there is still another four inches of image to each side that did not fit on this double-truck. Kodachrome II.

Pages 134-135 (left and right). Faces really tell the tale, and given glowing, tent-filtered sunlight and the enthusiasms of an auction crowd there for a purpose, the rest is easy. Nikkormat FTN, 105mm and 55mm lenses and both Kodachrome II and Ektachrome-X.

Pages 136-137 (right). Rodeos and parades lend themselves to the 105mm lens and the Nikkormat. Grey days are for Ektachrome-X, while bright sunlight makes me reach for Kodachrome II.

Pages 136-137 (right). Rodeo action is something else again. The 400mm Tele-Nikkor lens was tripod-mounted at the end of the roping area. A motordrive Nikon F was attached and a vast supply of film was on the ground beside me. It took me well into the morning to figure out just where the action would occur. And it took me the rest of the afternoon to shoot all the film. A surprising number of usable pictures resulted. Grey day, Ektachrome-X, lens wide-open.

Pages 140-141 (right). The occasion was the dedication of the reconstructed City of Refuge at Honaunau on the Kona Coast of the Big Island. The 105mm lens, Ektachrome-X film and the Nikkormat FTN were the tools used in this picture.

Pages 142-143 (left and right). The picture on the right came first, a portrait of one of the Hawaiian ladies of the Kaahumanu Society reflected in one of the faded mirrors circling the outside walls of Iolani Palace. With the reconstruction of the Palace presently underway I took one of the mirrors out onto the grounds. The photograph on the left is of the Palace itself reflected in the light from an evening sun. Both photographs were made with the 55mm Micro-Nikkor, wide-open, Kodachrome II.

Pages 146-147 (left). Grove Farm, the Kauai sugar plantation home of Miss Mabel Wilcox, one of the most gracious women in the Hawaiian Islands, lies low and rambling on a wide expanse of lawn outside Lihue, Kauai. A delightful woman to meet and talk with, Miss Wilcox made the few hours necessary for the portrait pass all too quickly. With the window light strongly directional, and a white bedsheet held up to reflect it into the shadow-side of her face, the flowers and painting of her parents — all were important elements in the photograph. Ektachrome-X film, the Nikkormat FTN tripod mounted, 35mm f/2 Nikkor lens.

Pages 146-147 (right). A straightforward picture of a graciously landscaped plantation house near Olaa on the Island of Hawaii. The 24mm lens provided the feeling of space, the palm trees covered with creepers acted as a frame for the picture. Nikkormat FTN, Kodachrome II.

Pages 150-151 (right). Climbing to the rim of Diamond Head Crater, my assistant and I lugged everything we could carry up the countless stairs to the World War Two observation post. As dusk approached, it was the little 105mm lens that turned the trick. Bracketed lengthy time exposures and Kodachrome II film. Nikkormat FTN.

Pages 152-153 (left). Well braced but handheld, High Speed Ektachrome, the 105mm lens on a Nikkormat FTN.

Pages 152-153 (right). Directly into the morning sun, High Speed Ektachrome to provide the film-speed needed to stop the 200mm lens down to f/22.

Pages 152-153 (far right). A simple record shot, 55mm lens, from a landing helicopter.

Pages 154-155 (left). Visual details and not fully formed photographs in their own right. The impact, if there, comes from the collective statement. Various lenses and films.

Pages 154-155 (right). 28mm lens, Nikkormat, from a helicopter.

Pages 160-161 (right). The movie set of the Mirisch Brothers film THE HAWAIIANS (no relationship to this book) was made for burning. A painstakingly detailed and accurate reproduction of Honolulu's old Chinatown section, it was spectacular when the burning came. With massive panavision motion picture cameras all around me, I felt a bit silly with my little Nikkormat and Micro-Nikkor lens and 36 paltry frames of Ektachrome-X. Not even smart enough to bring a motor drive unit with me that day, I had only one chance to get the photograph. I made it, to my everlasting relief.

Pages 160-161 (below). Movie extra, 105mm lens, Nikkormat FTN, Ektachrome-X.

Pages 162-163 (left). I have always liked to rely on natural light even when working exclusively in color. But one of the white reflecting umbrellas caught my eye in a local camera store and I bought it, along with two of the small Color-Tran floods. The chance to use it came the same day. The need to photograph the editor of one of the Chinese-language newspapers in the modern Chinatown of Honolulu. With Type-B Ektachrome, a tripod mounted Nikkormat FTN, and the 28mm lens, the single Color-Tran with umbrella reflector made child's play of the task.

Pages 162-163 (right). A variety of photographic problems. Two natural light 28mm shots, one 105mm natural light picture taken thru incense sticks out of focus, one with the 55mm Micro-Nikkor and umbrella reflected flood lighting, and one with direct flood lighting and the 105mm lens. See if you can match the technique with the correct images.

Pages 166-167 (left). The single orange, the black of the marble monument and the gold inscription are the three single elements that together make the statement in this photograph. 28mm lens, Kodachrome II, late late afternoon sun, Nikkormat.

Pages 166-167 (center). From the wings of the theatre a 400mm Tele-Nikkor shot of Japanese musicians. Out-of-focus images in the foreground add to the veiled quality. The image is reduced to the basic essentials, the faces of the players and the characteristic top end of the musical instrument. Nothing more. High Speed Ektachrome Type-B.

Pages 166-167 (right). The center-weighted exposure metering of the Nikkormat FTN makes this kind of photograph simple. A tree out of focus in the foreground, Kodachrome II film, tight framing on the subject, exposure for the gold panels on the side of the temple.

Pages 168-169 (right). I could easily claim to have known right along what this picture was going to look like when the film got back from the processor. Unfortunately that would not be the truth. I did respond to the image, focus, and trip the shutter. But I had no idea the tonality would be so delicate, the overall balance of the picture so exquisite. Every so often a picture like this comes along, and who's to say from where? I'm simply grateful to be able to claim it as mine. High Speed Ektachrome Type-B, Nikkormat FTN and tripod-mounted 400mm Tele-Nikkor lens.

Pages 170-171 (below and right). Many events occur in Honolulu that the rest of the community knows nothing of. A tiny article in the Honolulu Advertiser noted that there was to be a State Sumo Championship less than two miles from my house. It proved to be one of the most delightful afternoons imaginable, rich with photographic opportunities. And I was the only photographer present. Generally the shooting was with the 200mm lens, Ektachrome-X film and the Nikkormat.

Pages 174-175 (below). Not much to say about this picture except that using Ektachrome-X in bright sunlight is for me generally disastrous due to the extremely high saturation of color and contrast in this film. The red pants are a case in point.

Pages 174-175 (right). It was the beginning of the season for the little league teams, and their uniforms were cleaner than they would ever be again. There is no magic to this picture. It is simply a record shot of an appealing subject, clearly seen. And that is all that it needs to be. 200mm lens. Nikkormat FTN. Ektachrome-X on a cloudy-bright day.

Pages 176-177 (below and right). At elementary schools throughout Hawaii, Makahiki Day comes just before Thanksgiving. It is a day given over to things Hawaiian — offerings to Lono, hula dances and plays, all generally outside under a warm sun and cooled by the tradewinds. The children come with flower leis and dressed in Hawaiian costumes and it is a time of fun. The pictures on this spread were taken at an elementary school on the edge of Waimanalo, on the windward side of Oahu. 105mm and 200mm lenses, Ektachrome-X, Nikkormat FTN.

Pages 178-179 (left and below). From a fixed position I had tripod-mounted 400mm and 600mm Tele-Nikkors mounted to Nikkormats. The bright sunlight was just right for Kodachrome II, the graduation class at the University of Hawaii a good subject in that they couldn't easily move very much.

Pages 182-183 (left and right). The political rally was small and personal, a gathering of people who knew each other. There was a table full of potato chips and bowls of cheese dip and around the corner of the little park pavilion, a large washtub filled with ice and bottles of Primo beer. In a situation like this, anyone other than a local photographer is glaringly visible. To reduce visibility I generally work with only one Nikkormat and two or three lenses carried casually in an old World War Two gasmask bag. Having long passed thru the stage of wanting to look like the world's greatest professional photojournalist, I would now give anything to find a Nikon disguised as an Instamatic. The photography on this spread is straightforward and exceptional in no particular.

Pages 184-185 (left). It was the dawn religious service preceding the annual start of the outrigger canoe race from Molokai to Honolulu. The Governor was there to lend his presence to the event, as were others representing television, radio, and the newspapers. Standing directly in front of him I asked him to look at the camera. His look was wordless and stern and then softened a bit and then hardened again. I shot thru the sequence. The light from the rising sun was magnificent and strongly directional. Using the 28mm lens I was quite close to him. Something, a thought perhaps, pulled his attention away and he looked to his left and stared for the longest time into space. That provided the moment for the picture

reproduced here. Kodachrome II, Nikkormat FTN.

Pages 184-185 (below). Taken in the same morning light, three canoe paddlers. Nikkormat FTN, Kodachrome II and the 35mm f/2 Nikkor.

Pages 186-187 (left). Without my wife's help, this picture would have never come about. The opening of the State Legislature in Hawaii is always immensely colorful, a wealth of flowers and hulas and singing. This year it was to happen in the newly finished State Capitol Building. I'm very cautious about using a fish-eye lens. Most of the time they are used simply as a gimmick. So I arrived on the scene *without* the fish-eye and the minute I looked at what needed to be photographed, I was in big trouble. It was a natural fish-eye shot. No time to go home to get the lens. A frantic call to my wife and just minutes before the official opening she delivered the Nikon F body, the viewfinder and the lens itself. The rest was fairly routine. Lighting was natural and excellent, film was Type B High Speed Ektachrome, exposure was bracketed.

Pages 186-187 (right). All pictures were shot with the Nikkormat FTN, the 400mm Tele-Nikkor and the 200mm Nikkor, High Speed Ektachrome-Type B film.

Pages 190-191 (left and right). What is there to say? The 105mm and the 24mm used to get the simplest possible image. Kodachrome II.

Pages 192-193 (left). Converging verticals often add drama and the 24mm lens is a first choice for this kind of photograph. Kodachrome II, Nikkormat FTN.

Pages 192-193 (right). Again the 24mm lens, this time dealing with many curves at close range. Nikkormat FTN and Kodachrome II.

Pages 196-197. Structural steelwork is by its very nature dramatic. Set it off against a late afternoon sun, put a worker into the scene and it is very hard not to get an exciting image. A wide angle lens tilted upward was used to get converging vertical lines.

Pages 202-203 (right and left). Photographing people sitting around a table and talking is as close to a sedentary sport as you can get. The technique for getting interesting pictures of people at meetings is essentially one of boring them with your presence. First find a free chair at the table. Sit down as if you intend to stay there forever. Point your camera at your tablemates and if they glare at you or evince hostility, take their picture. Eventually you will condition them to ignore you and at that point put some film in your camera and begin shooting. Carefully evaluate the length and width of the table and then choose either your 105mm or 200mm lens. Whichever you choose you'll soon decide that the 135mm lens you didn't bring with you would have been ideal. These photographs were taken in a bad mix of artificial and natural light filtered thru yellowish drapes. Under these circumstances it is best to simply decide, on viewing the processed film, that the color you got is the color you wanted all along.

Pages 204-205 (below). When this picture was taken there was no thought as to how it might be used or even *if* it might be used. I was watching the threesome involve themselves with the white flower. When a subject fixes his or her attention fully on something external there is no room left in the moment for self-consciousness. If you have been following the action carefully enough you know exactly when to move in for closer photographs. Under most circumstances you can then bring the camera surprisingly close without disturbing the situation. 105mm lens, grey day, Nikkormat FTN and Ektachrome-X film.

Pages 204-205 (right). Back to meeting photographs, see note for pages 202-203.

Pages 208-209 (below). The prisms on this tiltmeter reflect a laser beam projected from the Volcano Observatory some few miles distant. The little flare of light in the picture was caught by moving the camera until the prismatic effect was visible in the reflex viewfinder of the camera. This picture would have been next to impossible to take with anything other than a single lens reflex or a view camera. Kodachrome II 28mm lens, Nikkormat FTN hand-held.

Pages 208-209 (right). We had hiked down a steep crater path doing our best to keep up with the scientists hoping to collect a lava sample from the edge of a newly forming lava lake. Mounting the 28mm lens on a Nikon F, the heat from the lava was close to unbearable. I'd frame and focus and shoot, and by then I felt as if the front of me was ready to burst into flame. By exposing my back to the heat I'd cool off my front and then swing around for another picture.

Pages 210-211 (left). The 28mm lens, Nikkormat FTN on a tripod and High Speed Ektachrome Type B pushed one stop for existing light exposure.

Pages 210-211 (right). In visually handling any subject, the 55mm lens gives an enormous number of options. This is one. Kodachrome II.

Pages 214-215 (right). In underwater photography, there are two very important things to remember. The first is that it is generally desirable to keep breathing as close to normally as possible. The second is that the widest angle lens possible is best. The reason is simply that the wider the effective angle of view, the closer you can get to your subject. The closer you get to your subject, the fewer suspended particles there will be in the water between you and your subject. And it is those particles which make many underwater photographs less-than-interesting, degrade their sharpness, and impair the color saturation of the subject. This picture was taken using the new Nikonos II with the 21mm Yashica f/3.3 lens, specially mounted and corrected for underwater use.

Pages 218-219 (below). One of the great breakthroughs in underwater photography of late was the development by Al Giddings of his beautifully designed Niko-Mar I housings for the motor-driven Nikon F. With interchangeable and fully corrected ports available for almost any lens you can think of, the housing boasts a through-the-lens viewfinder using Nikon's sports prism to provide the eye relief necessary for viewing the full ground glass image underwater while wearing a diving mask. Given that great benefit, the rest is quite easy. Ektachrome-X film, fully corrected 20mm Nikkor lens, motor driven Nikon F36.

Pages 218-219 (right). 105mm lens. Nikkormat, Kodachrome II.

Pages 220-221. The pictures of the undersea dwelling being towed into position for a test dive are straightforward record shots.

Pages 222-223 (left and right). Taking good underwater pictures is little different than taking good above water pictures. There are a few technical differences to master. The cameras "feel" differently. Thirty feet of

distance is your infinity. Color perception is at first, strange. For me the main difference is my sense of being in a hostile environment. Fear is always present when I dive at sea and I master it usually by twirling knobs on the camera and busying myself with the business of taking the picture. I've photographed underwater archaeology in swift currents a hundred feet down off the coast of Turkey; lived with Cousteau in his underwater village, Conshelf II, in the Red Sea, and with all that experience I dive in the open ocean with all the caution I can muster. The pictures were taken with the Niko-Mar I housing, sports-finder prism, fully corrected Nikkor 20mm lens and the Nikon F36 motor-drive unit. Ektachrome-X film.

Pages 224-225 (left and below). The Niko-Mar I, Al Giddings' camera housing, makes this kind of underwater photography quite easy. Ektachrome-X, fully corrected 20mm Nikkor lens, motor driven Nikon F36 body.

Page 229. I just have to tell this story. A friend related it to me and thus it is hearsay, but I quite believe it because it represents a way of thinking about photography. As the story goes, a photographer from one of our national magazines blew into the islands for an indepth coverage and chanced upon a burial cave on the Big Island. Going into the cave with limited lighting equipment he commented that he never takes pictures unless he has all the proper lighting equipment. Over the past few years I've gotten to the point where what really pleases me and tests my skills is to come upon a situation with a given lens on the camera, and then without changing that lens, to make the photograph from the enforced viewpoint of that particular lens or piece of equipment. The more rigid among us will insist that there is a *right* lens or lighting approach for every shot. I enjoyed trying to prove otherwise. Faced with *this* burial cave situation and a single battery powered flood light, I had the chance to put my photographic skills where my mouth is. Tripod-mounted Nikkormat with 20mm Nikkor lens. High Speed Ektachrome Type B, light purposely flared into lens for effect. Sylvania's Sungun provided the light.

Pages 230-231 (right). Shooting into the sun forces me into an old habit of bracketing my exposures. This picture was shot with the 24mm lens on Kodachrome II. Its essential quality is the sense of immense space one gets from the placement of the images of people and helicopter in the overall landscape.

Pages 230-231 (below). 55mm Micro-Nikkor lens, Kodachrome II, window light. Nikkormat FTN.

Pages 234-235. Some people are a delight to work with and photograph. Kauai's world-famous batik painter Jerome Wallace is certainly one. The most meaningful part of being a photographer for me comes in the relatively rare occasions when the taking of a photograph truly moves me into the orbit of another human being. Bridges are crossed, boundaries blurred and I always come out of the encounter much the richer for having involved myself. The camera is so often for me the excuse for being there, thus is at the heart of the experience. Yet once there, I paradoxically find myself not wanting to intrude upon the moment by using the camera. 24mm lens, Kodachrome II, Nikkormat FTN.

Pages 236-237 (left). Strongly directional lighting and a 24mm wide angle lens help make this shot of sculptor-painter Ed Stasack. With the camera mounted on a tripod there

was a great deal of time to work with Stasack in getting the exact balance of imagery desired. Ektachrome-X film.

Pages 236-237 (right). I wasn't aware of this photograph when I shot it, but one look at it on the light table convinced me that it has real impact for what it appears to be — but isn't. 24mm lens, Nikkormat FTN, Kodachrome II.

Pages 238-239 (below). 55mm Micro-Nikkor lens used for the protein bands photograph with the test tube lighted from below. Type B film. The other pictures were made on the microscope with Kodachrome II film. Specialized photography but very routine.

Pages 238-239 (right). At the University of Hawaii's Mees Solar Observatory on Haleakala, astronomers photograph the sun through different filters. By using filters, they can make visible certain temperature regions of the sun's atmosphere. The coronagraph used for this picture produces an artificial eclipse making more visible the corona itself. The filter used here is a 4 angstrom filter centered on 5305 angstroms. The green light is coming from highly ionized iron atoms at temperatures around two million degrees Kelvin. Exposure time was about 4 seconds.

Pages 240-241 (left). The large eruptive prominence is a hydrogen cloud. The picture was taken with the 10cm Dual Coronagraph through a five angstrom half width filter centered on 6563 angstroms and shows the cooler areas (approximately 7,000 degrees Kelvin) of this particular solar event. The aperture was f/30 and the exposure about a 1/5th of a second.

Pages 240-241 (right). The spectra was taken with the 25cm Coronagraph-Spectrograph at the Mees Solar Observatory. The telescope used has an effective numerical aperture of f/30, the dispersion on the spectra is 5.4 angstroms per millimeter. The color film used, Ektachrome MS or X showed peaks of sensitivity in blue-green and red making it impossible to get an even exposure across the full 16 inches of the focal plane. Exposure times ranged from a 1/15 to 1/60th of a second.

Pages 244-245 (below and right). I have long found it useful to possess a bit of brassnerve. On the morning of the great clam dig, up to my ankles in Kaneohe Bay mud and sinking ever lower, two very large local guys happened by and I asked them if I might stand on their shoulders to get a picture. They agreed. Kodachrome II film, the 24mm lens, and a Nikkormat FTN.

Pages 246-247 (right). Local surf photographer folklore has it that from a certain vantage point overlooking the big wave action of Waimea Bay one can measure a wave at 25 feet in height when the crest of the wave touches the horizon. This wave covered the horizon line and then some, and surf buffs have volunteered that this is the biggest wave ever photographed with a rider on it. The surfer didn't make it, by the way. For that matter, I didn't make it very well either, overexposing the frame, with the biggest wave of the year on it, by at least 1½ stops, at that. The engravers saved the picture by building back in the color.

Pages 250-251 (left). At a local golf course on the windward side of Oahu, this picture was simply irresistible. 400mm Tele-Nikkor, Nikkormat FTN, and Ektachrome-X film.

Pages 250-251 (right). Thanksgiving Day championship high school football game in Honolulu — and being on the field in front of this Farrington High School cheering section — was almost enough to cause permanent hearing loss. The 105mm lens filled the frame, Kodachrome II was the film and the Nikkormat FTN the camera.

Pages 252-253 (left). Grey day, Ektachrome-X film, the 200mm lens and a simple direct approach to the image.

Pages 252-253 (right). Although taken at widely separated locations, both pictures are of the same simple declarative type. The mainland-America beauty queen was taken on Kodachrome II, the young basketball player on High Speed Ektachrome.

Pages 254-255 (left and right). It was a festival for the Filipino community and involved a long early evening procession of adults and children holding candles. While there was still light I used Ektachrome-X and a slightly warming filter and got the picture of the beautiful girl on page 255. As it got darker, I put on the f/1.2 lens and loaded the Nikkormat with High Speed Ektachrome. Walking with the children I handheld for many many frames at ⅛th and ¼th-of-a-second. It was a calculated gamble that paid off with the pictures you see.

Pages 256-257 (left). The problem was how to depict the fact of Pearl Harbor without resorting to the constantly photographed Arizona Memorial. Spending Memorial Day in the National Memorial Cemetery of the Pacific inside Honolulu's Punchbowl Crater provided some answers. The grave marker picture was easy with the 28mm lens.

Pages 256-257 (right). The family being photographed at the grave of a loved one is by a Nikkormat FTN, tripod-mounted and with the 400mm Tele-Nikkor lens. Ektachrome-X was used for both photographs.

Page 259. A seventeen-foot stepladder got me up to a level with the statue. A 24mm lens filled the frame and provided a sense of the building behind. Kodachrome II film and the Nikkormat FTN.

Pages 260-261 (left and right). Both pictures are of a kind, large single-person images. The lighting on the caped and helmeted man is interesting and provides the real quality to the image. The large Samoan woman, however, is one of those rare images that is more than the sum of its parts. In massivity, in line, in color, and even in the interaction with the color in the background of the photograph — all these add to the photograph's impact. Shot with the Nikkormat FTN, the 200mm lens and, for the grey day, Ektachrome-X film.

Pages 262-263 (left). Both images Kodachrome II, and both shot with the 200mm lens. Nikkormat FTN.

Pages 262-263 (right). This is one of the "shoot-and-pray" pictures in which the light is just so impossible that you steady yourself against the nearest what-have-you, open the lens wide, and start the handheld ¼th-of-a-second exposures. To make matters worse, I was on the top of a short aluminum ladder I often carry so that I can get above the crowds. It was a none too steady platform but, as is sometimes my luck, I got the picture anyway. High-Speed Ektachrome, 35mm f/2 Nikkor, and a large hunk of just ignoring the fact that the picture couldn't be made that way. Nikkormat FTN.

Pages 264-265 (left and right). When your exposures are exactly right, Kodak color film gives you an extraordinary sense of plasticity in the tonality of the image. This picture of the clown is a case in point. It is on Ektachrome-X, and the tonality, even in reproduction, is exceptional. The Hawaiian is also an Ektachrome-X picture, this time with the 105mm lens and the Nikkormat.

Pages 266-267. We were at the end of the Aloha Week Parade. All the floats had pulled into the parking lot of Kapiolani Park, and people in costume were posing for the tourists and then getting ready to head home. One float depicting a luau was still in full swing, however. Fueled by their own gaiety, the laughter and dancing of the celebrants went on for a long time. The sequence of the old lady dancing a hula was taken with the Nikkormat, and the 105mm Nikkor.

Pages 268-269 (left). The Samoan dancers came in from both sides of the huge circle of islanders gathered for Samoan Flag Day celebrations in Ala Moana Park. I was as close to the center of things as I could get and still handhold the 200mm Kodachrome II, Nikkormat.

Pages 268-269 (right). The Samoan youngsters had made their own costumes of leaves and flowers. It was every bit as fine a dance performance as I had seen in Western Samoa itself. This wide-angle picture would have been helped enormously if I had brought along my two-step aluminum ladder. But I didn't have it and the picture is less good as a result. Ektachrome-X in bright sunlight (less than the best), 24mm lens on the Nikkormat.

Pages 272-273 (left and right). There were so very many usable photographs from this day. It began at dawn, a sunrise ceremony inside Diamond Head Crater, a Bedouin tent with prayer flags flying in the wind and the gentle sound of the sitar. And the day opened into an experience with thousands of young people relating to one another and to the place and the morning, and enjoying themselves. There was little that was ugly and much that was beautiful and it was a pleasure to simply roam and do my own thing. It was in some ways an almost perfect celebration of life in Hawaii.

Pages 274-275 (left). A Honolulu radio station sponsored a rock festival on a beach on the windward side of the island of Oahu, and these young islanders were two of the musicians who performed. The pictures are from very close up. The 28mm lens and the distortion one gets when moving in tightly was an effect that I very much wanted in the final pictures. Ektachrome-X, Nikkormat FTN.

Pages 274-275 (right). It was a bizarre performance, for me an excess in a day so beautiful it needed no excess. But she evidently felt like painting herself silver and she felt like dancing, and heaven knows her feelings caused me no trouble and even provided me with pictures. It was more of the Sunshine Festival from the previous page. Ektachrome-X, 105mm lens, Nikkormat FTN.

Pages 276-277 (left). Art Park, another festival for the young, provided the opportunity for these pictures of young girls. The blue image is on infrared color film and like most gimmick photography would probably have looked better if shot normally.

Pages 276-277 (right). Again the 400mm Tele-Nikkor demonstrates its incredible usefulness for theatre photography. Low light level, one stop push on High Speed Ektachrome Type B, during a Japanese Noh play in Honolulu. Nikkormat FTN.

Pages 280-281. Wo Fat's is a very well-known Chinese restaurant whose windows overlook the main street of Honolulu's Chinatown. It was the night of the Chinese New Year celebration and firecracker smoke was heavy everywhere. With camera on tripod I climbed out a window of Wo Fat's main dining room and set up on a rickety overhang directly over the street. I was close enough to use the 105mm lens and through the smoke got the picture on this spread. Nikkormat FTN. High Speed Ektachrome Type B pushed to 320 ASA.

Pages 282-283 (left). The old lady was lighting incense sticks in a Chinese Temple at the entrance to Honolulu's Foster Botanical Garden. High Speed Ektachrome, 28mm lens, and the Nikkormat.

Pages 282-283 (right). More from Chinese New Year celebrations on Maunakea Street in Honolulu. I had arranged with the Chinese Chamber of Commerce to have every fourth light bulb in the string of colored lights, hung for the occasion, replaced with a photoflood. Shooting High Speed Ektachrome Type B at 320 ASA, and using the 35mm f/2 wideangle, I had no difficulty getting the pictures.

Pages 284-285 (right). An Okinawan dance, High Speed Ektachrome Type B pushed one stop, Nikkormat FTN and the 400mm Tele-Nikkor lens on tripod.

Pages 286-287 (left and right). I go away from a situation like this feeling very depressed. Even with four or five rolls of film in the bag I'm certain that I failed to get what my eye told me was there. I had raced all over the beach that night, guessing at exposures, bracketing wildly, using the wide-angles and normal and super telephoto lenses, trying to blanket the situation. And true to form, I went away depressed. For no reason I can think of the pictures turned out; they even became the closer for our book. High Speed Ektachrome Type B, 320 ASA, and one well-worn Nikkormat on a unipod.

The Principal
HAWAIIAN ISLANDS

22°

0   25   50
STATUTE MILES

MAP SYMBOLS

—— Roads	✈ Commercial Airfields
══ Dual Lane Roads	✈ Military Airfields
---- Trails	Coral Reef
69 Highway Numbers	Swamp
HI Interstate	← Warm Currents
	Elevations in Feet

⌐ Special Points of Interest
□ Other Points of Interest
Heiau (Ancient Temple)
Petroglyphs (Rock Paintings)
∴ Ruins
see the Illustrated Atlas of Hawaii

Channel

MOLOKAI
Ilio Point
Moomomi
Kepuhi
Kalaupapa
Mauna Loa Hoolehua •Halawa
+1381
Kaunakakai 4970+
Kamalo •Pukoo

Pailolo Channel

•Honokohau

Pohakuloa Pt.
Kaena Point Kaanapali Wailuku •Pauwela
1799 5788 •Kailua
LANAI Lahaina + Kahului
Kaumalapau Lanai City Olowalu **MAUI**
+3370 Waiakoa •Honomaele
Palaoa Point Kamaole •Hana
Manele Bay 10023+ Red Hill
Kukui Point Nuu •Koali
KAHOOLAWE •Keoneoio
+1477

21°

Alenuihaha Channel

Upolu Point
Hawi •Kohala
Mahukona
Waipio •Kukuihaele
Honokaa
Kawaihae 5505+ •Paauilo
Waimea •Laupahoehoe
(Kamuela)
•Hakalau
Kiholo• Mauna Kea
13796
Mahaiula• •Papaikou
Puuanahulu• •Pohakuloa Hilo
Kailua• •Keaau (Olaa)
H A W A I I
Kealakekua Kainaliu •Mountain View
Mauna Loa Pahoa
Honaunau• 13680 Kilauea Crater •Pohoiki
4077+
•Kalapana
•Koa Mill
Milolii• •Pahala
Ninole
Waiohinu• •Naalehu

Ka Lae (South Point)

20°

19°

157°   156°   155°   154°

Acknowledgement

A project such as THE HAWAIIANS is helped along by many people, from the very humble to the highly distinguished. To thank them all by name for their faith and commitment, their generosity and patience, would be beyond our eloquence and space. They know who they are, and we are deeply appreciative of their help.

A project such as THE HAWAIIANS becomes possible only through the statesmanship and support of a group of organisations and a handful of people in them. We admire and are grateful for their investment in a society of which they are wise enough to know themselves a part. Without those listed here, our vision could never have been given form:

ALEXANDER & BALDWIN, INC.
AMFAC, INC.
ALOHA AIRLINES, INC.
BANK OF HAWAII
BOISE CASCADE RECREATION COMMUNITIES GROUP
CASTLE & COOKE, INC.
C. BREWER AND COMPANY, LIMITED
DILLINGHAM CORPORATION
FIRST HAWAIIAN BANK
FIRST INSURANCE COMPANY OF HAWAII, LTD.
'A NATIONAL GENERAL COMPANY'
FOREMOST DAIRIES-HAWAII, LTD.
HAWAII NATIONAL BANK
HAWAII VISITORS BUREAU
HAWAIIAN AIRLINES
HAWAIIAN ELECTRIC COMPANY, INC.
HAWAIIAN TELEPHONE COMPANY
HAWAIIAN WESTERN STEEL LIMITED
HILTON HAWAIIAN VILLAGE
HONOLULU GAS COMPANY, LIMITED
HONOLULU STAR-BULLETIN
INTERISLAND RESORTS, LTD.
KAISER CEMENT & GYPSUM CORPORATION
KAISER HAWAII-KAI DEVELOPMENT CO.
MALIA HAWAII INC.
PAN AMERICAN WORLD AIRWAYS
SIGNAL PROPERTIES, INC.
STANDARD OIL COMPANY OF CALIFORNIA
THE HAWAII CORPORATION
THE HONOLULU ADVERTISER
THE ILIKAI HOTEL AND MAKAHA INN affiliated with
CAPITAL INVESTMENT OF HAWAII, INC.
THEO. H. DAVIES & CO., LTD.
TRADE WIND TOURS OF HAWAII
UNITED AIR LINES
WORLD AIRWAYS